THE PROOF OF GOD

THE PROOF OF GOD
The Debate That Shaped Modern Belief

LARRY WITHAM

ATLAS & CO.
New York

ATLAS & CO. PUBLISHERS
15 West 26th Street, 2nd floor
New York, NY 10010
www.atlasandco.com

Distributed to the trade by W. W. Norton & Company

Printed in the United States

For credit information, please see page 209.
Maps by Sergey Ivanov

Atlas & Co. books may be purchased for
educational, business, or sales promotional use.
For information, please write to info@atlasandco.com.

LIBRARY OF CONGRESS CATALOGING-IN-PUBLICATION DATA
IS AVAILABLE UPON REQUEST

ISBN-13: 978-0-9777433-6-0

13 12 11 10 09 08 1 2 3 4 5 6

INTERIOR DESIGN AND TYPESETTING BY SARA E. STEMEN

Contents

Anselm's Fool

NEARLY a thousand years ago, a monk named Anselm, prior of the Bec monastery in Normandy, France, turned to his Old Testament for the exact phrase he was after:

> *The fool says in his heart, 'There is no God.'*

The text is from Psalms, and it would inspire history's most famous "proof" for God's existence.

Each day at the Bec monastery, monks received a pound of bread, two hot bowls of gruel, and whatever vegetables, fruit, and cheese—or surreptitious meat, forbidden by the Benedictine Rule—could be found. But in search of the proof, Anselm had neither an appetite nor a desire to sleep, according to his biographer, the monk Eadmer. When the proof finally illuminated Anselm's mind during matins, the Psalm-reciting night prayers, he wasted no time in putting it down.

Anselm found a well-lighted place to work and rolled up the sleeves of his coarse, black-dyed frock, worn by all Benedictine monks. In Latin, he began writing the proof down with a sharp stick on a wax tablet, the legal-sized notepad of the day. From here, the only account of this struggle to obtain the proof, and to answer the fool definitively, would take on the quality of legend.

Eadmer, author of the fifty-thousand-word *Life of Anselm*, reports that Anselm had to write the proof down twice, maybe three times. His first draft was stolen and his second was found shattered on the stone floor—no one knows why. On the third round, Anselm ordered a scribe to copy the proof in ink, on animal-skin parchment.

In his proof, Anselm argues that when the fool acknowledges the idea of God—"something than which nothing greater can be thought"—he concedes that such a perfect being has to exist in reality as well as in the mind. It is logically "greater" to exist in mind *and* reality, rather than just in mind. A chapter later, Anselm adds that it is logically "absurd" to try to think of such a God as not existing. By definition, God's existence is necessary.

Anselm made his claim around 1078, and the first response to it wasn't long in coming. A little south of Anselm, at another monastery in the French countryside, the monk Gaunilo read his proof as it circulated in a very limited edition, and, putting stylus to wax, sent Anselm his rebuttal, titled *On Behalf of the Fool*. Gaunilo was pleasant but blunt. Just because an idea exists in the mind, he told Anselm, it doesn't have to exist in reality. Does a Lost Island conceived as the most perfect of its kind exist in some ocean simply because Anselm thinks of it? Gaunilo, a bent figure in his eighties, had seen youthful enthusiasm before (even though Anselm was already forty-five). If he followed the logic of Anselm, Gaunilo suggested, "I should find it hard to decide which of us I ought to judge the bigger fool."

Anselm was undiscouraged. Back at the refectory table, his appetite restored, he resumed conversing with his fellow monks—though talk during meals was forbidden by the Benedictine Rule—and took up his wax tablet to reply to his antagonist Gaunilo. When a person hears the word God, Anselm insisted, the reality of God "is understood and is in the mind." Once God was in the mind, the proof must work.

With this exchange, one of the most famous debates in Western history had begun. Critics and friends called Anselm's proposal marvelous or preposterous, too simple or too complicated. Anselm, seeking truth by reason alone, knew he was treading on new ground and assured contemporaries that he was not "an arrogant modernizer," even though he was developing a hybrid of Christian and classical philosophy that the world had never seen before. Anselm's approach to proving God is now known as the Ontological Proof, using a term that the German philosopher Immanuel Kant crafted from the Greek *ontos*, or "being."

Anselm offered two kinds of ontological proof in his essay and elaborated further in his reply to Gaunilo. His attempt to find a "single" argument for God's existence was already giving way to a variety of arguments, all of them originating "in the mind"—that is, they begin with a premise, operate on logic, and resemble mathematical formulae. They are a priori arguments: they arise from self-evident propositions and require no evidence outside the mind. (Consider, for example, Aristotle's premise that A cannot be non-A, or Euclid's axiom that two parallel lines never cross—both are results of pure logic but are nonetheless applicable to the physical world.)

Anselm's was an age in which the effort to understand the world by reason was beginning to challenge the word of ancient authorities. The tradition of quoting exclusively from the church fathers came under siege as medieval philosophers began to smuggle Aristotle into their discourses on theology, philosophy, and logic—a development that would come to be known as scholasticism. This Greek logic, called "dialectic" for its analytic powers, became Christianized as it was applied to belief in God, the Bible, and doctrines of the early church. Anselm was surrounded by the first generation of these new dialectical Christian thinkers, who viewed the cosmos as a unity presided over by an almighty Creator. The scholastics fleshed out this connected universe, showing how deeply it was linked, one part to another. Anselm, too, was inspired by a belief in a corresponding harmony among the mind, God, physical things, logic, and spoken language. This gave him the confidence to find a rational proof for God.

When Gaunilo sparred with Anselm, the idea of a connection among all things was a matter of dispute. Gaunilo believed in God, but he rejected the idea that the mind could grasp the ineffable Being. For Gaunilo, the mind could know only the world of things. Where Anselm spoke of the concept of God, Gaunilo talked of a Lost Island. For Gaunilo, all knowledge came from "things" outside the mind, an approach to evidence that philosophers call *a posteriori* (versus a priori). Anselm argued for the primacy of mind, Gaunilo for the physical senses.

When his proof of God was published, Anselm titled it *Faith Seeking Understanding,* later shortened to *Proslogion,* or "authoritative address." We don't know whether he changed Gaunilo's mind. Few people read Anselm's proof in the century after his death; only in the thirteenth century did it spark wide interest. The most prominent voice to emerge in the "things" camp appeared in the fourteenth century. He was William of Ockham, a Franciscan monk who maintained that logic could not prove God's existence. Ockham challenged Anselm's assumption that the universe is connected by essences and principles, linked by invisible substances that could be discussed in terms of reason and logic.

For Ockham, essences and substances were not real things at all, but merely "names." He thus revived a kind of ancient heresy called *nominalism* (the Latin for "names" is *nomina*). If all the essences are merely words, or hot air—"*flatus voces,*" as one early nominalist said—

then what is truly real? Ockham gave the nominalist answer: only *things* are real, at least to the human mind and senses. Nominalism after Ockham swept Western thought. It pitted the belief in "only things" against a belief in unseen essences that connected and organized every part of God's creation. In time, this cutting away of metaphysical essences from philosophy earned Ockham's logic the fierce term *Ockham's Razor* (some would say Ockham's chisel or eraser, for the image of that day was of razor-wielding monks scraping ink mistakes off the sturdy, expensive parchment). Ockham's Razor reduced philosophical and scientific problems to simple "things," which excluded a priori proofs of the unseen world.

By the seventeenth century, an entire epoch beyond Ockham, nominalism was still going strong. It presented a special challenge to a Catholic philosopher in France, René Descartes, who revived the type of proof used by Anselm and tried to establish once again that the mind could know God and the essence of reality by reason alone. Descartes's century was also a time of growing philosophical skepticism, so he deployed his proofs of God in a way that would defeat the skeptics and offer a modern alternative to the nominalist cosmos. Descartes's proof of God, nearly a dead ringer for Anselm's (a family of "proofs" later called the "Ontological Proof" of God), sought to restore certainty by describing a universe in which all things—logic, experience, thought, and

God among them—were connected in a single reality. Like Anselm, Descartes believed in the primacy of mind and declared that it was trustworthy, whatever the skeptics said. Moreover, the mind itself was a "thinking thing" that could conceive even God "clearly and distinctly."

This story of the Ontological Proof proceeds in a great arc, stretching from Anselm to Ockham to Descartes. For reasons that will become clear, Anselm was called "the father of scholasticism," Ockham the "first Protestant," and Descartes the "first modern philosopher." They carried the debate on the Ontological Proof into the present, shaping modern belief with two possible views of the world. One, following Anselm and Descartes, views the mind as deeply connected to the universe, particularly by reason, and able to harmonize God and the world into one integrated whole. In the nominalist view of Ockham—essentially a materialist view as it was handed down in history—human knowledge is limited to knowing the universe as a vast assemblage of things—atoms, trees, hats, town meetings, prime ministers, cups of coffee, planets—not a metaphysical world of essences that can be grasped by human reason or insight. Most of all, nominalism denies the possibility of proving God.

DESCARTES'S eventual renown did not convert all the great minds of Europe to his "Cartesian" philosophy or his proof of God. But his dedication to rationalism was very much in vogue when, in the late 1600s, the philosopher Gottfried Leibniz gave the proof another boost in history. Leibniz, an elaborate dresser who made his living at the pleasure of royal courts, had rivaled Isaac Newton as inventor of calculus (a method of mathematics). He also had an Anselmian vision of a harmonized universe. Leibniz believed it was possible to prove God's existence by reason alone—that is, with his new-and-improved Ontological Argument, for which he gave credit to precursors thus: "What Descartes has borrowed from Anselm is very beautiful and really very ingenious."

This talk of proofs, which was now circulating among such noted thinkers as Leibniz and Baruch Spinoza, a Jewish lens grinder who lived in Holland, put another philosopher, Immanuel Kant, on edge. Eventually Kant rejected the ultimate power of reason, and in *The Critique of Pure Reason* (1781) he offered "On the Impossibility of an Ontological Proof of the Existence of God," arguing that reason falls into contradiction when used to answer questions about God, eternity, and other ineffable topics, and advising that ethics is the more certain road to God. Kant had given the Anselmian argument its enduring title (the "Ontological Proof"), but he was hardly the last to dismiss its validity. A decade after Kant's death, the philosopher Arthur

Schopenhauer, a notorious pessimist, added his own acidulous critique: "The famous Ontological Argument is really a charming joke."

But the joke would not die. At the turn of the twentieth century, the future British philosopher Bertrand Russell was persuaded, at least for a moment. Like Anselm at matins, he had an epiphany: It was 1894 and he was walking down the narrow, cobblestoned Trinity Lane at Cambridge University, having just bought a tin of tobacco, when it struck him. "Great Scott, the ontological argument is sound," he exclaimed, throwing the tobacco tin in the air and catching it.

But despite the proof's attempt to present a universe in which the mind, God, and physical things are all connected, the modern force of nominalism carried the day. The story of Russell and his contemporary, the Austrian philosopher Ludwig Wittgenstein, illustrates that nominalist victory. Russell gave up on the Ontological Proof and became a champion of the philosophy of logical analysis. This "logical positivism" did away with metaphysics, asserting that reality is made up of facts and words, and that is all. Russell confessed to wielding Ockham's razor in order to reduce all things and words to the minimal vocabulary of pure mathematics.

Wittgenstein, whom Russell and others had brought to Cambridge, took this logical simplification even further. He used the razor of logic to cut reality down to *just* words. In the process, he declared that

the positivist project was ultimately hopeless: it was
not possible to line up all the facts of the world and
give each one a word. In his last work, *Philosophical
Investigations*, published soon after he died in 1951,
Wittgenstein declared that reality is like a set of rules
for "language-games." For him, finally, there were no
philosophical problems: there was no point in asking,
'Does God exist?' It all came down to a puzzle of language. Whether "God" was invoked by theologians or
atheists, determining the nature of the word and the
idea was increasingly seen as nothing more than a language game.

The debate isn't over. Logical analysis and language games have banished God from the ivory towers
of academia, but believers and doubters continue the
debate in the streets. For the believer, the Anselmian
option presents God as something "in the mind," found
by reason, commonsense, intuition, or insight. For the
atheist or agnostic (who is invariably a nominalist),
the universe is an assemblage of things—and if reality
consists only of things, then where is the thing called
"God"?

The Ontological Proof has defined this debate
in Western thought. Over a millennium, it has sharpened the wits of believers and nonbelievers, beguiling
some and infuriating others. Even today, it retains a
strange and magnetic allure, as do the philosophers
who have engaged with it. They are players in the story
of "faith seeking understanding," in the story of belief

and disbelief. As Leibniz notes, Descartes "borrowed" the Ontological Proof from Anselm, a monk who lived almost a thousand years before Russell threw his tobacco tin into the air.

CANTERBURY

PARIS

BEC CLUNY

AOSTA

LYONS

ROME

AGE OF ANSELM
1033 - 1109

CHAPTER 1

The Logic of God

A NSELM was born in the Italian border town of Aosta, high in the Alps and a point from which the cultures of Europe had long diverged. To the west was France, the land of Anselm's destiny and home to his mother's clan. To the east lay the rest of what we now call Italy, culture of his father's birth, and a place Anselm would visit only late in life. In Roman times, Aosta was the last city on the Italian frontier of the empire, guarding Saint Bernard Pass. Roman ruins filled the steep Aosta valley. On all sides, rocky peaks reached into the clouds, and a young Anselm must have imagined how high up was the dwelling place of God himself.

Emperors viewed the mountains differently. They were ramparts against enemies and borders to guard. When Anselm was born in 1033 CE, the Holy Roman Emperor (the king of Germany) was shuffling this alpine territory. The emperor annexed the lands west of Aosta and called them Burgundy. Emperors were important figures, but in a feudal age local rule made all the difference. In Aosta and elsewhere, counts and bishops collected taxes, while monarchs and popes remained distant. For Anselm's part of the world, the leading religious figure was the abbot of the great Cluny monastery, just beyond Burgundy in France.

During the twenty-three years that Anselm lived in Aosta, he learned of the world from merchants and travelers through the great pass. Though his mother had blood ties to Burgundy's House of Savoy, it was a declining family line. Anselm had no inheritance. Only a provincial education, his parents told him, would gain him a career, which in the eleventh century meant a church appointment. The ladder climbed from canon to administrator and even to bishop. At the local church, Anselm probably served as a clerk, which allowed him an early opportunity to test his academic acumen. Behind that modest desk, he also began to think about a great world beyond the Alps, a world known as Christendom.

Medieval feudal society was a fragmented affair, held together as much by religious imagination as by actions of government. Kings wore Christian relics in amulets around their necks, adding to their air of mystical power. The pope, no more than an Italian aristocrat, asserted a benign authority by sitting on Saint Peter's chair. The church calendar was filled with pageants and ceremonies. The nobles and the masses were brought together by pilgrimages to Spain, parades of relics, celebrations of miracles, and trials of heretics.

The monastery system was the nerve center of society. It was founded on the Rule of Benedict, a regime of piety in daily life; all monasteries of that era were Benedictine. They arose by the thousands, and one appeared in Aosta as well. The city had an abbey, or monastery church, and a cathedral.

When Anselm informed his father that he wanted to become a monk, he was met with stern resistance. Not even the abbot could change his father's mind. Anselm nearly starved himself in protest, as he later told his biographer, Eadmer. He was driven to his vocation by a dream in which, high in the mountains, God had interviewed him and a steward brought him the "whitest of bread" to eat after his long climb. Family resistance, however, quelled this first religious ambition. As Eadmer tells us, Anselm "gradually turned from study, which had formerly been his chief occupation, and began to give himself up to youthful amusements."

The monastery was still the best avenue to literacy and interesting work. The high-ranking families knew this well. They used the monastery churches for their family rituals, from birth to death. The nobility showered monasteries with contributions and asked prayers in return. When such families ran out of land to divide among children, or if daughters lacked suitable husbands, then children were sent to become monks and nuns. Monasteries became like private colleges and religious houses, but they never lost their broader social functions. They were centers of charity, way stations, and hospitals. Monasteries produced the finest art, crafts, musical instruments, and books.

In Anselm's lifetime, two great monasteries stood out, one in France and the other in Italy. Although Italy's rocky-perched Monte Cassino monastery took pride of place in papal tradition, the newer one in France represented the future. The monastery of Cluny, founded by a pious duke a century before Anselm's birth, was one of the largest religious complexes in the world during his time. Cluny had become the center of reform for all Benedictine monasteries in the land.

After Anselm's mother died, he lost his piety and his diligence. As Eadmer put it: "The ship of his heart had as it were lost its anchor and drifted almost entirely among the waves of the world." He saw nothing to keep him in Aosta, so in 1056 he packed his bags and went off to explore the world. From the Alps, he descended into the great Rhone Valley, which runs from today's Lake Geneva to the Mediterranean Sea. He saw a new Europe in the making. As he wandered west, he crossed paths with knights, Cluniac monks, scholars, and fortune seekers migrating south, on their way to Spain on pilgrimage. Not all were devout. The Cluniacs produced a new kind of specialized monk, a military monk who rode on a horse, upheld codes of chivalry, and was an effective killing machine when necessary. In a few more decades, these Christian forces would "reconquer" Spain, with Toledo as the prize—a city that would reveal to the Latin theologians a whole new body of ancient Greek philosophy and science.

On his path through France, Anselm saw horses pulling new heavy-duty plows, breaking the hard clay soil for wheat, barley, millet, and oats. He traveled past scenes where two fields were planted and one left fallow—the new technique of crop rotation—and he gazed up at hillsides with miles of black furrows and green seedlings, with orchards nearby. He left no travel accounts, but in later life his biographer recounts Anselm's references to "fields and woods" and "mills," the dynamos of medieval life.

Windmills and water mills ground flour wherever a river or beast of burden was at hand, for bread was the main staple of the common diet. Ordinary people ate dark and coarse bread (rye, barley, oats, millet, and rougher wheat) and the well-to-do the white loafs, produced from refined wheat. It was no accident that Anselm had dreamt of the "whitest bread" in God's royal court. Without famine, the population grew dramatically, as the new cities that rose up all over Europe would attest to in the next two centuries.

In the Rhone Valley, Anselm saw the remarkable number of Roman ruins scattered about, now being put to good use. They were fast becoming the foundations of churches built by Burgundians, French, and Normans, who were Christianized Vikings. Their combined architecture, later called Romanesque, was castle-like with windowless blunt walls, great arches, and cylindrical towers. As one monk described the buildings: "Each Christian people strove against the others to erect nobler ones."

Anselm traveled for three years, keeping a close eye on the architecture—always a sign of opportunity. A cathedral spire usually indicated a school. In those days, an aspiring student had two options: training as a lawyer or as a clerk. They could study either at a monastery or at a secular liberal arts school, where they were taught grammar, logic, and rhetoric based on a small set of Greek and Roman classic texts that had survived—with Cicero for rhetoric and Aristotle for logic. Amid the noisy cities, these schools often convened at a cathedral. Their anchor was a master teacher who organized classes, guided readings of texts, and oversaw academic disputation.

As schools, the monasteries had one leg up. They had discipline. Monasteries enforced not only prayer, meditation, and penance, but also reading, work in the scriptorium, and manual chores in shops or fields. The Rule of Benedict espoused obedience, and under its firm hand monasteries produced the West's book culture. As a kind of productive penance, monks with good penmanship spent hours making new copies of old books, a tireless, hand-cramping, and frustrating task. They illuminated manuscripts with colorful glosses and drawings. The monasteries raised the animals whose skins produced the best parchment (also called *vellum*): baby calves and sheep were best, but there were also deer, antelope, goat, and piglet (for small sheets). Monks split and scraped skins, producing several grades of parchment, remarkably durable, and showing a rich grain and hair markings that gave it its valued texture and warmth.

With parchment, they made both sacred and profane books, preserving the works of church fathers—such as Augustine, Ambrose, Bede, Cassian, Eusebius, and Gregory—and the Greek and Roman pagans alike. They first pressed pages between boards, and then invented covers and bindings, which made it possible for the first time to stack books on shelves. Books were precious. At a wealthy monastery, a monk might be issued one book per year, while the others were chained to desks. The arduous copying filled monasteries with the greatest works of the past millennium. Those monasteries that failed to thrive became tombs, hiding their treasures in dank stone rooms and wooden cabinets. When the musty tombs were finally opened in the fifteenth century, the books spawned the Renaissance.

In a Normandy cathedral town called Avaranches, at the very edge of civilized Europe, Anselm heard of a much-revered liberal arts master. His name was Lanfranc, and he was a fellow Italian, trained in Pavia, a center of legal studies. Lanfranc had become a master of the city's legal courts by the age of twenty-five. In 1042, he migrated to Avaranches, and in that frontier city began to consider the calling of the monastic life. After years of prominence in the secular world, he left Avaranches to join the small, barely known abbey of Bec near the Risle River. The Bec church was a century old; it had become a monastery in 1034, when the local noble-man, Dom Herlwin, invested his money in the project and became Bec's abbot. Bec had only a few monks when Lanfranc arrived, mostly young children of local lords. So he launched a unique growth strategy in an age when all Benedictine monasteries were growing: he opened a secular liberal arts school. It was funded by local nobles, and even the papal court in Rome sent clerks for training under the formidable Lanfranc.

When Anselm heard of this man, Lanfranc was in his fifties and the best-known religious figure in Normandy. Not least, he was said to be the religious advisor to William, the young and ambitious Duke of Normandy. Anselm decided that this was the place to start his formal education, so he turned his back on the frontier and traveled toward Bec, arriving sometime in 1059. He enrolled at the monastery's secular school.

Anselm, now wise to the ways of the world, was full of calculation. He wanted to accomplish something but not enslave himself to the rigors of places such as Cluny, with its long hours of menial labor and military-style regimen. If he had headed into Italy from Aosta he might have found a monastic community with a more contemplative and charitable bent. He did a careful cost-benefit analysis, typical of any ambitious young man at a career crossroads. When Anselm compared the life of a monk to that of a wandering student, the former looked better. As a monk he would at least not "lose the reward of his labour." After much deliberation, he said to himself:

> Well then, I shall become a monk. But where? If at Cluny or at Bec, all the time I have spent in study will be lost. For at Cluny the severity of the order, and at Bec the outstanding ability of Lanfranc, who is a monk there, will condemn me either to fruitlessness or insignificance. Let me therefore carry out my plan somewhere where I can both display my knowledge and be of service to others.

As with so many of Anselm's words, these were his reflections offered later in life, speaking to his loyal biographer, Eadmer. Covering up for his subject's unmonkish ambition, Eadmer often embellished Anselm's own statements, making humility the priority. He quotes Anselm: "So put aside your rebelliousness and become a monk in that place where, rightly and for God's sake, you will be lowest of all, and where you will be most insignificant and be held in less esteem than all others. And where can this be? At Bec, of course."

Lanfranc was in need of a protégé of Anselm's talents. He welcomed Anselm's inquiry and took him on a journey through the north woods to Rouen to gain approval from the local authority, Archbishop Maurilius. It was 1060 and Anselm was twenty-seven. He took the vows of piety, simplicity, and obedience and stuck with them for the next fifty years. Anselm had reached a turning point in his life, but it was an interior one, little connected to the great institutional convulsions of the church. In another decade or two, Anselm would begin to confront the real world outside the monastery. Already, as he turned inward as an apprentice monk, the church was in upheaval. The papacy in Rome was struggling to emerge from political irrelevance.

FOR at least two centuries, popes had been pawns caught between Italian nobles and German emperors. A few years before Anselm left Aosta, he may have heard travelers' tales about a new mood in Rome: the popes were not going to take it anymore. The church first showed this resolve in the person of Pope Leo IX, who had ties to Cluny and surrounded himself with brilliant Cluniac advisors. The most important of them was the German monk Hildebrand. As a lieutenant, he was the chief architect of the papal future. Once the new papal strategy and system were in place, Hildebrand himself became pope, and by building upon this centralization of power, he began to face down secular rulers and create a church of bureaucracy and law, thereby becoming the "greatest" pope in centuries.

In the quarter century between Leo's election and Hildebrand's (as Gregory VII in 1073), business as usual in Rome had changed. Under Rome's guidance, the Latin Church broke with the Greeks. (They finally excommunicated each other after centuries of uneasy diplomacy over the pope being the top bishop in Christendom.) The new papacy also extended its control in the Latin Church by way of legates, letters, and councils. The 1059 Council of Rome declared that only cardinals could elect popes, thus excluding princes, kings, and even emperors. Rome also stripped secular rulers of church ownership and required clergy to be celibate. But reform had its risks. Now that the papacy had excluded German emperors from a role in papal elections, the pope needed a new political alliance, having so boldly offended the German throne.

In its early history, the papacy had allied itself with Byzantine emperors. That all changed in the eighth century, when the papacy rebuffed Byzantium and chose the Franks, or Germans, as its military protectors. Now the pope wanted complete independence. The most opportune path was to renew an alliance with the Normans, who ruled southern Italy and northern France (Normandy). In the year that Anselm arrived at Bec, Pope Nicholas II reached out to his most important Norman ally, William, the Duke of Normandy.

The year was 1059 and both Pope Nicholas and Duke William were in a hurry. Pope Nicholas wanted to launch his reforms while the new German emperor, Henry IV, was still just a boy. Duke William, who had family ties to the throne in England, believed he deserved that position when the aging king died. To invade England successfully, William needed to be in good standing with Rome. So Pope Nicholas and Duke

William came to one of the most delicate, and notorious, arrangements in the medieval annals of church-
state cooperation.

To help bring it about, Pope Nicholas turned to
the obvious intermediary, Lanfranc, the master of Bec
and spiritual advisor to William. The pope summoned
Lanfranc to the great Council in Rome. The first issue
at hand was church acceptance of William's adulterous
marriage. The duke had married into the ruling family
of Flanders, which protected his northern flank, before
divorcing his first wife. Pope Nicholas felt he had no
choice but to bless the irregular second marriage. In
return, the Norman army became the pope's traveling
bodyguard.

Lanfranc was no doubt a disinterested figure,
caught as he was between these two great powerbro-
kers. But opportunities opened up for him as well.
William showered him with favors for the rest of his
days. First he summoned Lanfranc to Caen, a burgeon-
ing city, to open a great new monastery and preside at
a new cathedral. Three years later, William was ready
to fulfill his military ambitions and invade England.
As every English schoolboy knows, in 1066 William
the Conqueror turned England into a French colony.
He eventually installed his favorite, Lanfranc, as archbishop of Canterbury.

These events changed Anselm's life. He was
elected by his fellow monks to take Lanfranc's place
when he left for Caen. It was a fast advancement for

Anselm, who had been at the Bec monastery for only four years, and it stirred some jealousy. But he assuaged the conflict by a show of generous leadership. As soon became clear, Lanfranc and Anselm were very different people. Lanfranc was an administrator and builder. Anselm recoiled at bureaucracy. He begged Archbishop Maurilius to let him quit, but received the reply: "And if you are ever called to a higher office you are by no means to decline it." He endured his duties at Bec for thirty-four years, and between administrative headaches, he found his true talent.

BY joining Bec, Anselm gained a front-row seat to some of the great theological debates of the day. The age of scholasticism had dawned, and in the struggle to merge the ancient Greek heritage of Aristotle with medieval Christian dogma, the stakes were high: the future of Christian theology hung in the balance. How much of Christian thought would operate in the pagan modes of logic and reason, and how much would retain the elements of faith and revelation?

The question was exploding across Christendom, and the hottest point of contention was the "real presence" of Christ in the bread of the Eucharist. Belief in His real presence was a dogma. But the Eucharist debate opened the church door to using Aristotle's logic as a way to make theology more rational. Until now, most theological assertion was based on citing authority: the Bible, Saint Augustine, the Creeds, or the early church

fathers. The liberal arts had introduced new tools, and
these included grammar, rhetoric, and logic—the so-
called *trivium*. In the great Eucharist debate, the logical question was how the spiritual Christ and physical
bread could occupy the same space. The rhetorical or
semantic question was, 'What did the Bible mean when
Christ said he was the bread?'

The debate came to a head at the Council of Rome
in 1059. The church called in two advocates, one orthodox and the other innovative. The first was Lanfranc,
who defended the orthodox position of *transubstantiation*: that the bread turned into the body of Christ, even
though it looked like bread to human eyes. The other
disputant was Berengar of Tours, a respected theologian who defended a contrary solution. Lanfranc and
Berengar were old friends. They had both been secular
scholars and masters of the trivium before becoming
monks and theologians. They had also become masters
of the dialectic, the new reasoning method that gave
scholastic theology its edgy character. In the words
of the colorful chronicler, William of Malmesbury,
Lanfranc "sent out his pupils into the world belching
forth dialectic."

Berengar had stirred the theological crisis by his
insistence on grammatical logic. In some ways, this
made him the more conservative of the two. He con-
tended that both Christ and the bread occupied the
same reality, for that was the literal claim of the phras-
ing in the Bible and in early church writings. Words

had real meanings, Berengar argued. Having two things occupy one space was indeed a mystery; but the "real presence" of Christ in bread is just that, a mystery.

Lanfranc was no less logical in his solution, but he had chosen to draw upon the logical categories of Aristotle, not on a semantic argument. More than a thousand years earlier, Aristotle had founded the discipline of formal logic. He gave it its first rules and laid out categories by which to organize reality. One of the few surviving works of Aristotle was his short manuscript the *Categories*, which, as scholars, both Berengar and Lanfranc knew well. But this was just the dawn of scholasticism, and even Lanfranc did not mention Aristotle's name—the great thinker was a pagan. He only used Aristotle's logic.

The *Categories* defined real things as having a permanent essence, or "substance," but also having changing qualities or appearances, called "accidents." No two substances could share the same space. The Eucharist was the same, Lanfranc said. After consecration, its one substance was Christ's body, although its accident looked like bread. Only by the mercy of God were human eyes spared seeing the actual divine flesh. The Eucharist debate foreshadowed what was to come, for scholasticism was forever caught in deciding which was more real, the words or the categories? Berengar and Lanfranc paved the way for the scholastic era, and Anselm would soon march into it using his own novel approach.

The debate was a victory for Lanfranc and transubstantiation. Berengar's solution seemed to diminish the Eucharist, the ingredients of which were viewed as being entirely Christ after consecration by the priest. His teaching was condemned, and his name tarnished. Overall, however, the papacy was not excited about this intrusion of the liberal arts into dogma. The papacy was more interested in having Lanfranc train secular clerks. This was the age of the "lawyer popes." In their vision of a vast papal administration, there was a great need for skilled legates and bookkeepers, not argumentative theologians. But Lanfranc was far more interested in theological scholasticism, which to Rome seemed like a slippery slope into unnecessary analysis of theological dogma.

For good reason, Lanfranc habitually avoided mention of Aristotle and the rules of the dialectic. He used other phraseology, "thus hiding [his] art" behind the kinds of words used by ancient authorities such as Augustine. Lanfranc's students understood the revolution that was taking place. They were excited by the new dialectic and realized it was showing up even in Lanfranc's biblical works, such as his *Commentary on the Epistles of Saint Paul*, which analyzed the logic, rhetoric, and grammar of the holy apostle. Lanfranc showed how even Paul was a dialectician, using logic, premise, order of argument, and conclusion. He argued his doctrines by resolving conflicts between two assertions and by "disproving opposites."

Anselm had soaked up this dialectic from Lanfranc. His mature mind was born into a new age that had room for both the trivium and Christian faith. Above all, he adopted the worldview of Aristotle, although even Anselm did not mention the pagan philosopher's name. The name he mentioned most was Saint Augustine—an even greater influence on Anselm, who would come to be called "the second Augustine" for his prolific writings. But the first work that Anselm ever completed was straight out of Aristotle's *Categories*. By 1063 Anselm had written a little book on logic called *De Grammatico*.

Such a project required two things: the tools and setting of the scriptorium, and a library. Fortunately for Anselm, Bec had both. Lanfranc had turned Bec into a center for copying, correcting, and repairing manuscripts. Monks used wax tablets for notes, drafts, and compositions, and wore them dangling from their girdles. Anything worth keeping from the wax was written down by skilled scribes in ink. The Bec library probably contained the monastery standard for the time: the Bible, Rule of Benedict, and as much Augustine as possible.

Of the pagan works, Aristotle was the most important, though only his *Categories* text had survived in the Christian West. The *Categories* was a mere sliver of the entire corpus of Aristotle, still to be uncovered, but it shaped the dialectical thinking not only of liberal arts, but also of early Christian scholasticism. Dialecticians strove to make theological doctrines more intelligible. They tried to analyze physical mysteries of the faith, such as Christ in bread, original sin passed by physical birth, and how a physical hand, when it ordains a priest or invests a king, passes on a spiritual power. The dialectic looked for hidden dimensions, such as "substances," and it also looked for every logical way that matter and spirit could coexist.

Wisely, Anselm stayed out of these great controversies when he wrote his first book. Composed as a dialogue between a teacher and his truculent student, *De Grammatico* reviewed Aristotle's substances and accidents—the essence of things and their visible qualities—and the principles of logical grammar. Anselm loved to play with grammar, but even more so with the basic tool of Aristotle's logic, later called the *syllogism*. The Greek term means "a reckoning together" or "summing up" of two claims. The syllogism was the main engine of the dialectic, and its use grew throughout the Middle Ages. The syllogism could reveal the structure of thought through symbols. For example:

A is equal to B.
B is equal to C.
Therefore, C is equal to A.

Or the syllogism could show the connection between things.

Man is mortal.
Socrates is a man.
Therefore, Socrates is mortal.

The syllogism established the pattern of first premise, second premise, and necessary conclusion. As its use grew, so did the debate over its two essential parts: was the first premise self-evident (for example, man is mortal) and was the second premise appropriate (Socrates is a man)? When the syllogism was used to prove the existence of God, as Anselm would attempt, the two premises were the hotly disputed issues. To take one form of the Ontological Argument:

> *First premise:* By definition, God is the being with
>   all perfections.
> *Second premise:* Existence is a perfection.
> *Necessary Conclusion:* Therefore, God possesses
>   existence.

Syllogism, as a tool, seemed limitless. But Aristotle offered one other kind of tool, which looked at what was probable, possible, impossible, or necessary. (This is called modal logic.) As Aristotle argued in the *Categories,* "It is not possible for fire to be cold or snow to be black." The whole web of Aristotelian logic presented a universe that could make sense to a Christian believer: a world in which God, things, logic, and words all corresponded harmoniously. Aristotle's logic also explained why the whole range of things that humans could say about the universe included some things that were *necessary*, others that were *possible*, and still others that were *impossible* (such as cold fire).

Anselm exploited both the syllogism and modal logic to maximum effect. He argued that God's existence was necessary—God was the necessary first category to explain the world as it was seen and experienced by the human mind. Put another way: God's nonexistence was impossible. There had to be a first, perfect, infinite category for all other categories (such as "man," "mortal," and "Socrates") to exist. This was the new tortured syntax of Western philosophy, and it lasted for the next thousand years.

IT was 1063 when Anselm finished writing *De Grammatico*, just as Lanfranc departed for Caen, which now thrust Anselm into the No. 2 leadership role as prior at Bec. For the next three years in Normandy, as Anselm busied himself with administration, Duke William prepared to fulfill his greatest ambition: to invade England and take the English throne. When the summer of 1066 arrived, William's army still lay stalled on the Norman coast as poor winds made crossing the English Channel impossible. But in October, as the fogs and squalls lifted, William launched his attack.

He crossed the channel and met the rival claimant to the throne, King Harold, on the battlefield at Hastings. The pope allowed William to fly the papal banner, which probably unnerved the pious Harold. The English took a high ridge, creating a wall of shields. But as the high-shot arrows of the Normans crashed down, the line broke. On horseback, Normans stormed forward with axes, swords, and pikes, taking Canterbury, London, and Windsor.

The conquest of 1066 barely altered the life of a small valley like the home of the Bec monastery. While France and England fought, Anselm sat in his room and wrote. He composed devotional works and probed theological problems; according to Eadmer, "[h]e attained such a height of divine speculation, that he was able by God's help to see into and unravel many most obscure and previously insoluble questions about the divinity of God and about our faith, and to prove by plain arguments that what he said was firm and catholic truth."

By 1075, he had compiled enough of his devotional writings to publish them as two separate collections, his *Prayers* and his *Meditations*. To publish, in those days, was to translate texts from wax tablet to multiple copies on parchment, stacked or bound. Anselm was becoming known outside Bec as a writer, both by his letters and these new publications. Of those written over a lifetime, four hundred of his letters have survived. Most come from his time at Bec.

His early letters, while always preoccupied with teaching truth, even a bit pedantically, were effusive and emotional. Anselm's central theme to monks was

friendship. Over a period of fifteen years, he wrote
of this trait to all manner of men—bishops, students,
monks, rulers—frequently addressing them as "most
beloved" and referring to "embraces," "kisses," and
"longings." This was before the advent of romantic letters as a literary style in Europe, but not too long before;
later translators found themselves a little embarrassed
by his purple prose. But this was likely to have been
Platonic affection only. It was spiced with youthful
ardor, rhyme, and a dash of ecstasy. As Anselm wrote
to one monk named Henry, a rather rough-hewn and
secular fellow, "I do not doubt that we both love the
other equally. I am sure that each of us equally desires
the other, for those whose minds are fused together in
the fire of love, suffer equally if their bodies are separated by the place of the daily occupations...."

Anselm wrote with cloying words but stern
doctrine. Severity toward himself and his soul filled
his letters, *Prayers*, and *Meditations*. "I am the poorest
and basest of *homunculi*," he wrote in a prayer of self-
abasement to Saint Peter, "I try to stir up my dull mind
and hold it back from vanities which destroy it." Anselm
sent his prayers and meditations to patrons and aristocratic women interested in piety. In a letter to Adelaide,
an unmarried aristocrat who was semi-monastic, he
wrote as a "friend of your soul," recommending seven
prayers and one meditation, the content of which he
described: "In it, the soul of the sinner briefly exam-
ines itself; despises what it finds; is humbled by what

it despises; in humiliation is smitten with terror of the Last Judgment, and breaks into tears and lamentation."

For monks he had this advice: "The purpose of the prayers and meditations which follow is to excite the mind of the reader either to the love of God or fear of God, or to self-examination."

His work was beginning to get around: royal patrons and monasteries began to request copies of his *Prayers* and *Meditations*. These efforts at compilation would culminate, many years later, in a thick volume of his writings that he delivered to Countess Matilda of Tuscany, a famed military woman (who rode at the front of her army!) and a defender of a strong Gregorian papacy. The portrait of her receiving the collection from Anselm is one of the enduring images of him in the medieval manuscripts.

WHILE Anselm focused on literary matters at Bec, the emperor and the pope were inching toward a final showdown.

For nearly thirteen years, since 1061, the church had declared Alexander II as its pope. But Alexander's election had excluded the German emperor, so the emperor had chosen his own "anti-pope," Honorious II, and sent the German army south to install him on the papal throne in Rome. Thus, Alexander II's papal administration was often on the road, as medieval papacies frequently were, trying to avoid German armies. But the tables were about to turn. The papacy now had its own military allies, the Normans, and in 1073 the church elected Gregory (Hildebrand, the German) pope by acclamation. Gregory "the Great" would confront the German emperor with all the might the papacy could muster.

As Pope Gregory, Hildebrand invented the "modern" papacy. He had come to the throne with thirty years of experience, rising from papal chaplain to treasurer and principal counselor. Now he created a legal monarchy and elevated canon law above secular codes. He changed the papacy from "vicar of Peter" to "vicar of Christ" and his *Dictatus papae* decreed twenty-seven truths, among them the dictate that "only the pope's feet are to be kissed by all princes" and not the feet of kings or emperors. He fired recalcitrant prelates, audited bishoprics, and called councils. Every bishop pledged loyalty to the new papacy and every archbishop came to Rome to receive the symbol of his authority, a woolen neck vestment called a *pallium*.

In Germany, meanwhile, Henry IV believed himself still in charge as the Holy Roman Emperor. His view was this: emperors installed popes, and popes, in humility and gratitude, blessed emperors. Since this clearly wasn't happening, Henry IV deposed Pope Gregory, who excommunicated Henry in return. Europe waited to see what would happen next. The traditional German response was to invade Rome, and as the year 1077 arrived, that was indeed a plan Henry considered. The pope knew his history well. He traveled north to the fort of Canossa in the Apennine Mountains, a castle owned by the feisty Countess Matilda, who had also spent her life warring with the German emperors. The winter snows began to cover north Italy. Nevertheless, Henry IV organized an army and headed south, crossing into Italy by the Cenis Pass, where Anselm had begun his journey into French lands.

This was not to be a castle siege or great bloodletting. As the story is told, Henry had come to repent—with his army in the rear, just in case he changed his mind and needed to make the pope do the repenting. But Henry followed the higher road. He begged the pope to lift the excommunication, standing barefoot in the snows of Canossa for three days, it is said, before Pope Gregory let him inside to receive the papal blessing.

While Henry and Gregory rattled sword and scepter, Anselm had already begun to work on his two most famous books, the *Monologion* and *Proslogion*. Ever after, the idea of God was commonly spoken of as "something than which nothing greater can be thought." It took Anselm three years, the most creative of his life, to develop this claim in his proof.

CHAPTER 2

"I Began to Wonder"

A NSELM was in his mid-forties in 1077, the year Gregory and Henry met in the snowy Italian mountains. At the Bec monastery, he was in the middle of a three-year project, a collection of writings that focused on the greatest scholastic puzzle: whether God could be explained or proved by reason alone.

Already, Anselm's harmless little *De Grammatico* had put him at the head of a youthful revolt, at least compared to Lanfranc, who wrote like a footnoting lawyer. Anselm dashed off phrases like, "But listen! I think I hear the distant rumble of a contradiction." His letters were filled with effusion and rhymes, but even his theological works, such as the *Proslogion*, opened with a kind of whimsy that would shock Lanfranc: "Come now, insignificant man, fly for a moment from your affairs, escape for a little while from the tumult of your thoughts. Put aside now your weighty cares and leave your wearisome toils."

In contrast, the old school of Lanfranc insisted on quoting ancient authorities. Anselm wrote in that same conservative Augustine tradition, but he used words of his own invention. Armed with the dialectic, he took distinctions to a degree of precision that even Augustine never achieved. At Bec during these three years, each day was still ordered by the drone of routine: early hours, repetitive prayers, work in the gardens, workshops, and scriptorium, and then more prayers followed by sleep. When he could, Anselm reached for the wax tablet at his side and found a corner in which to escape his relentless chores.

EADMER'S years of eyewitness reporting, and his eye for detail, dates, and melodramatic flourishes, made his biography of Anselm one of the best-narrated in early medieval times. As often happens with biographers and subjects, though, it was a relationship that couldn't end well. At first, Anselm was cooperative, sharing with Eadmer every detail of his life and thoughts. For seven years Eadmer observed Anselm in his role as archbishop, taking notes with vitality and candor, especially on the politics of the era. But near the end, Anselm ordered him to destroy the biography, recoiling at its vanity. Eadmer destroyed only one copy. The biographer, "utterly confounded" by Anselm's directive, decided to take on a "sin of disobedience." He explained after Anselm's passing:

> I did not dare to disobey him flatly; but I could not face the destruction of a work on which I had spent so much time. So I obeyed him in the letter by destroying the quires [folded parchments] on which

the work was written, having first transcribed the contents onto other quires.

When Anselm learned of his ploy, all trust was lost. It was history that gained. Anselm had revealed everything to Eadmer, including the story of the proof of God. In the story of the Bec years, Anselm was doing some personal justifying as well, for he probably felt guilty about devoting himself to metaphysics when the monastery had so many practical problems to solve, from leaking roofs to stray herds and tiffs between monks. But as Eadmer notes, metaphysics was "where his interest lay." In the *Monologion*, Anselm offers his own explanation of why he wrote:

> Some of my brethren have often and earnestly asked me to write down, as a kind of model meditation, some of the things I have said, in everyday language, on the subject of meditating upon the essence of the divine; and on some of the other subjects bound up with such meditations.

The *Monologion* and *Proslogion* were written back-to-back between 1075 and 1078. They were two sides of a coin, the second completing what Anselm had started in the first. The first book was "made up of a connected chain of many arguments," according to Anselm. The second book attempted in "one single argument" to summarize them all. Anselm combined every stylistic spin that he knew. Logic guided both works. But he wrote the first in the form of a self-interrogation, much as he had done in his *Meditations*. He wrote the second as a prayer. The first was Anselm's conversation with his own mind, as if he were an actor in soliloquy on stage. The second was Anselm's conversation with God. Together, the *Monologion* and *Proslogion* offer a proof of God's existence using no other evidence but the logical workings of the mind—reason alone, much as when Aristotle said A cannot be non-A, and Euclid said that two parallel lines could never cross.

Anselm did not dive into his proof of God from the first word. The *Monologion*, for example, stopped short of a 'God' argument. It argued only that all the good qualities in the world come from a single, transcendent source. The *Monologion* surveyed these essences: life, reason, health, justice, wisdom, truth, goodness, greatness, beauty, immortality, incorruptibility, immutability, happiness, eternity, power, and unity. The "necessary conclusion," Anselm maintained, is that a "supreme essence" made possible all that is good in the world. "Since, then, the supreme nature is not composite at all, and yet really is all those good things, it is necessary that all those good things are not many, but one."

This was hardly a daring assertion. But Anselm was speaking in a new parlance. He departed from Lanfranc and the ancient authorities, and staked his belief on the new logic. Anselm wanted to grasp God "simply by reason alone," for that was the very role of the mind: "The rational mind may be the only created thing that is able to rise to the task of investigating the supreme nature." Anselm knew this was a risky proposal, so he set up his rhetorical defenses. "If, then, someone thinks that I have said here anything which is either too modern, or which departs from the truth," he offered, "I would ask them not to denounce me as an arrogant modernizer or maintainer of falsehood." His supporting witness was "Blessed Augustine."

When Anselm completed the *Monologion* in about 1077, its piecemeal arguments were strung out across eighty paragraph-like chapters. Nervously, he sent it to Lanfranc for approval and a title. Lanfranc's response was cool. His only comment was that Anselm had not sufficiently quoted Augustine. Anselm replied: "However often I look over what I have written, I cannot see that I have asserted anything that is not found" in ancient authorities. Despite his self-effacing letters to Lanfranc, Anselm was confident in what he had achieved. So he cast about for his own title. First he chose "an example of meditating about the substance of faith" (*Exemplum meditandi de ratione fidei*), and then "Monologion on the substance of faith" (*Monoloquium de ratione fidei*). Finally, "for the sake of greater convenience," he recalls, he distilled it to the pithy *Monologion*, or "soliloquy."

Looking over his eighty brief paragraphs with his students, Anselm sensed there was still more to be done.

He hadn't yet delivered the philosophical coup de grâce. As he recalls,

> I began to wonder if perhaps it might be possible to find one single argument that for its proof required no other save itself, and that but itself would suffice to prove that God really exists, that He is the supreme good needing no other and is He whom all things have need of for their being and well-being, and also to prove whatever we believe about the Divine Being.

This was the agenda of the *Proslogion*, "another small book." But unlike its predecessor, the *Proslogion* was born in passion and legend. Finding the single argument for God's existence, Eadmer says, "gave him great trouble, partly because thinking about it took away his desire for food, drink, and sleep, and partly—and this was more grievous to him—because it disturbed the attention which he ought to have paid to matins and to Divine service at other times."

During prayers, Anselm's mind darted from one point of logic to another. Like so many future mathematicians who would sit uncomfortably at their desks for hours in search of an equation that comes full circle, he was in search of a 'proof.' At one point, Anselm thought he was being tempted by evil. Was it right to try to grasp God with his finite logic? Even Augustine and Lanfranc counseled acceptance of mystery. But Anselm could not resist. He completed his intellectual quest sitting in a dim, stone-walled monastery chapel. Candles flickered, monks dozed, and spiders crawled on walls streaked with rain and mildew. Anselm, no young man anymore, sat on a hard oak bench. The drone of someone reciting the Psalms wafted in the damp air. We don't know the day of the week or even the season. But as Eadmer reports,

> Then suddenly one night during matins the grace of God illuminated his heart, the whole matter became clear to his mind, and a great joy and exultation filled his inmost being. Thinking therefore that others also would be glad to know what he had found, he immediately and ungrudgingly wrote it on writing tablets and gave them to one of the brethren of the monastery for safe-keeping.

This was not as easy as it sounded. First the wax tablets were lost or stolen. Anselm wrote another draft while his thoughts were fresh. He placed it in a "more secret" chest by his bed. But the next day, the monks found the tablets broken and strewn on the floor. They collected them and took them to Anselm, who, fearing a total loss, ordered "in the name of the Lord" that the text be copied onto parchment. From this material, Eadmer recalls, Anselm "composed a volume, small in size but full of weighty discourse and most subtle speculation," soon called the *Proslogion*, or authoritative address.

The "single argument" of the *Proslogion* occupied only the first three of twenty-six chapters. In the future, philosophers would call this the Ontological Proof, for it was an argument to "prove" the existence of the great Being who preceded all other beings. Anselm built his argument on a premise he had inherited from the Greeks and his fellow Christians: the mind, God, things, and even words all corresponded in a harmonious way, if only they could be presented logically. As Anselm saw it, the existence of God is necessary, for all of reality fits together just so, and can be known by any rational mind willing to follow the logic.

The *Proslogion* is unique in medieval literature. Anselm neither quotes authorities nor relies excessively on Scripture. He begins with a story from the Old Testament, in which there is a "fool" who declares, "There is no God." Anselm builds his proof by analyzing this simple scenario. The words of the fool are enough for Anselm to produce three ground rules. First, the fool uses the word *God*. Next, by using that word he must have had the idea of God *in his mind*. Based on these first two elements, the fool claimed God's nonexistence.

Anselm defines God as "something than which nothing greater can be thought." By referring to God, the fool must have this conception of God *in his mind*. But then the fool denies that God exists outside his mind—in reality. This is the contradiction that proves God does exist. To be the greatest thing, the idea of God must also exist outside the mind. By the mere cognition of 'God,' the fool has made God's existence necessary. It is impossible for this Being not to exist in reality. As Anselm states confidently, "Certainly this being so truly exists that it cannot even be thought not to exist."

Anselm believed that words had consequences, as he had already argued in his *De Grammatico*. Words must speak of a reality, and so it was with the *God* word. The foolishness of the fool had begun when he first thought of God and said the word *God*, for by that very thought and action, the fool had logically concluded that God must exist. It was impossible for God not to exist, if he were "something than which nothing greater can be thought." Centuries later, Bertrand Russell offered this synopsis:

> We define 'God' as the greatest possible object of thought. Now if an object of thought does not exist, another, exactly like it, which does exist, is greater. Therefore the greatest of all objects of thought must exist, since, otherwise, another, still greater, would be possible. Therefore God exists.

But Anselm also spoke in terms of the impossibility of conceiving of God's nonexistence. The philosopher Norman Malcolm, a student and biographer of Ludwig Wittgenstein, did his best to explain this side of Anselm's logic:

So if God exists His existence is necessary. Thus God's existence is either impossible or necessary. It can be the former [impossible] only if the concept of such a being is self-contradictory or in some way logically absurd. Assuming this is not so, it follows that He necessarily exists.

For better or worse, modern philosophers who do everything in symbolic logic have rendered Anselm into mathematical formulae. In formal logic, every premise and element in a proof is turned into a symbol so they can be manipulated like numbers in a long mathematical equation. To explain the twenty-eight steps in an Anselmian-type proof of God, for example, one logician explained step four with the following formula, where symbols stand for "the fool," "can imagine," and "exists in reality," among many other factors:

$$(\forall y)(((\exists x) x My \& \neg Ey) \to (\forall z) Ez \to z Gy))A$$

Whatever the merit of Anselm's Ontological Proof, it has become what historian R. W. Southern calls the "only general, non-technical philosophical argument" from the Middle Ages that continues to occupy the interests of modern philosophers.

WHEN a copy of the *Proslogion* found its way to the Marmoutiers monastery, just fifty miles south of Bec, the prior there was well acquainted with the author.

The prior's name was Gaunilo, and we only know of him today because of a little tract famously called *On Behalf of the Fool*.

Gaunilo was much older than Anselm. Perhaps in his eighties, he knew flights of youthful speculation when he saw them; and now comes Anselm with a proof of God! As Eadmer recounts, Gaunilo "found fault with one of the arguments in [the *Proslogion*], judging it to be unsound." Gaunilo attached his rebuttal to Anselm's piece, circulated it, and a friend of Anselm's passed *On Behalf of the Fool* back to Bec. Anselm "read it with pleasure," thanked his critic effusively, and responded with a counter-rebuttal.

Gaunilo called the *Proslogion* a saintly work. Then he attacked on two fronts. First, Gaunilo questioned whether a finite human being could possibly have the idea of an infinite God "in" the mind. "I can so little think of or entertain in my mind this being," Gaunilo said, "as I can think of God Himself." Human knowledge is limited to a world of things. When the *God* word is spoken, the mind recognizes a "verbal formula," Gaunilo went on, so God exists in the mind "only in the sense that I understand what is said." In this way only, God is "in my mind and not in any other sense."

This was subtle material. Even in the modern age of neuroscience, it is unclear what is "in" the mind, whether it be the impression of objects, understanding of mathematics, holding a concept like infinity, or even having memory upon memory, which neuroscience cannot fully locate or explain. Gaunilo rejected all this mind-probing of Anselm's. With the common sense of a baker or table-maker, Gaunilo offered a classic refutation of the Ontological Argument: he said that only things (like blocks of pine or pounds of wheat flour) can be talked about with any certainty: the mind can know only finite things. From these, the mind creates analogies for the infinite, such as God. In this first rebuttal, Gaunilo felt quite confident. "So much for the claim that that supreme nature exists already in the mind."

Gaunilo had a team of capable scribes at the Marmoutiers monastery. He would write his thoughts on the wax tablets, and then the monks would get to work, putting it onto parchment with a rich, black ink. These parchments, like all letters of business, would be bundled up and stuffed into the mail bags of the day, carried by monks on foot, by mule or, if a monastery was prosperous, by a swift horse. Not a few monks in their black frocks and cowls were seen galloping across the medieval landscape on horseback.

After reading Gaunilo's parchment tract, Anselm turned to his own wax tablets. In his rebuttal, he relied on a tradition of his age. Medieval theology often argued that the infinite God can be known by negating what is finite. In other words, God is *not* what is finite, and by acknowledging this fact the mind gradually develops a full concept of deity—of what God *is*. Anselm argued that the mind can understand all worldly things as having a beginning in time and a place. These things can be real or imaginary, a tree on the hillside or unicorns and centaurs in the imagination of a monk who paints one into an illuminated manuscript. Because these things have a beginning and end, they are not God. Furthermore, if the mind can think of anything greater than a particular thing—call it X—then X is not God. That leaves God well-defined in the mind: God has no beginning, no time, and no place. "Surely then," Anselm concludes, "that-than-which-a-greater-cannot-be-thought' is understood and is in the mind to the extent that we understand these things about it."

But Gaunilo had a second argument against Anselm—what modern thinkers might call a "thought experiment": somewhere in the ocean exists a perfect island, called the "Lost Island" because it is so hard (or impossible) to find. This island is so perfect that no other island could be conceived as better. The word "island" enters the mind, Gaunilo says, but does that mean it really exists? "If, I say, someone wishes to thus persuade me that this island really exists beyond all doubt, I should either think that he was joking, or I should find it hard to decide which of us I ought to judge the bigger fool."

Anselm's response was jocular, but with a little bit of edge. The topic is not a finite island, but a uniquely infinite being, he maintained. The two are hardly comparable. Gaunilo was talking about a particular kind of being (an island), while Anselm was talking about

Being itself (God). "For 'that which is greater than everything' and 'that than which a greater cannot be thought' are not equivalent for the purpose of proving the existence of the thing spoken of."

For all the uniqueness of Anselm's *Proslogion*, even an innovator borrows, and admits it to varying degrees. There is no record of Anselm's sources, but the Bec library shelves offer a clue. He may have read Seneca's *Quaestiones Naturales*, in which the philosopher claimed that God's physical "magnitude" is "that than which nothing greater can be thought." Or he could have been paraphrasing—without attribution—the Roman statesman Boethius, the sole translator of Aristotle at the time, who had written in his *Consolation of Philosophy* that "nothing can be imagined better than God."

But as in all else, Anselm drew mostly on Augustine, who had a lot to say about God being the greatest of things. In *On Free Choice of the Will*, he cites the "fool" in Psalms and asks his student, Evodius, if God could be proved to such a disbeliever. Poor Evodius, facing the formidable Augustine, falls back on faith. Then Augustine helps the boy out, saying,

> Now you had conceded that if I proved the existence
> of something higher than our minds, you would
> admit that it was God, as long as there was nothing
> higher still.... For if there is something more

excellent than the truth, then that is God; if not, the
truth itself is God. So in either case you cannot deny
that God exists.

Like his philosophical predecessors, Anselm saw
the universe as having "degrees of being," from highest
to lowest, from greatest to least. He lived in a hierarchical society, manifest in kings, popes, princes, and bishops on earth, all overseen by a majestic God. There was
a "fitting" order to things, fitting to a noble God and
a universe that gave order to the mind and to human
conduct, making the cosmos a beautiful place.

This ordering was the basis of Anselm's proof. The
highest degree is to exist in the mind and in reality. A
bit lower is to exist only in reality, and lower still is to
exist only in the mind—to be a fiction, a unicorn or
centaur in the imagination of the monk painting a gro-
tesque on a parchment page, or carving it onto a cathedral rain spout. The world of real beings also fell into
degrees. The *Monologion* presents the supreme essence
as "that than which absolutely nothing is better." From
there it is all downhill. Things are "not all of equal value,
but differ by degrees," Anselm wrote. "For the nature of
a horse is better than that of a tree, and that of a human
more excellent than that of a horse, and to doubt it is
simply not human."

Anselm must have felt some satisfaction that the
Monologion and *Proslogion* were being read. But when

Abbot Herlwin of Bec died in 1078, Anselm was forced back to the things of this world. He was now Abbot Anselm, a title attended by heavy responsibilities.

AS an actor in the world, Anselm is almost as mysterious as his lofty metaphysics. Eadmer was good at everything but physical descriptions, so none remain. But the man Anselm can be cobbled together with a few facts here, imagination there, and some of the more colorful accounts of Eadmer. Finally, there is the Anselm revealed by his letters, prayers, and meditations, which usually sound like religious press releases, but nevertheless show glimpses of his personality.

Born in Italy, Anselm may have had a swarthy complexion, but this is sheer speculation. The only thing for sure is that, once a monk, he tonsured his hair and proudly wore a shiny pate. From this point, the artists take over. In the manuscripts of his era, he was an abstract, cartoon figure: big round eyes and holy repose. Later artists portrayed him as an old man with swept-back white hair and a hooked nose. Inevitably, he became statuesque, a man of strong jaw, firm gaze, modeled hair and beard, and broad shoulders: witness the Italian figurines and stone and bronze statues at Canterbury and any church that came to be called St. Anselm.

The man Anselm is more truly known from his stories, perhaps. In both his letters and talks, he mimicked New Testament parables, substituting the wine, mustard seed, and wheat stalks of Palestine with things of his own time: bear-keepers, wheat millers who labored beside rushing rivers, and knights, weary of battle, who took the monk's vows. Eadmer also made his life a lesson, in good hagiographic style. Once, a group of malicious hunters with dogs taunted a cornered rabbit that had sought refuge under Anselm's horse; as he snapped the reins and bolted down the road, Anselm turned back and shouted, "So it is with the soul of man!" (Evil spirits also "stand round without mercy, ready to seize it and hurry it off to everlasting death.") Naturally, the dogs were scared off by Anselm, and the rabbit leapt to freedom.

Another time, Anselm came upon a boy torment-ing a bird, tying a string to its leg—a scene that offered a clear lesson about the soul. "Consider likewise how the devil plays with many men, whom he catches in his toils and drags into various vices," Anselm said, pleased to see the bird pull free, leaving the boy in tears. Wax also played into Anselm allegories. Young people, like soft wax, should be treated well and guided, before they harden into sin and cynicism:

> Take a man who has been sunk in the vanity of this world from infancy to extreme old age, knowing only earthly things, and altogether set in these ways. Converse with such a man about spiritual things, talk to him about the fine points of divine contemplation, show him how to explore heavenly mysteries, and you will find he cannot see the things you wish him to. And no wonder. He is the hardened wax; his life

has not moved in these paths; he has learnt to follow other ways.

Eadmer showed little restraint. In his hagiography, Anselm cast out demons, healed the sick, had prophetic visions, crossed the sea in a leaking ship, and even prophesied that a hungry traveler would catch a particular type of fish in the river: "If anyone doubts whether Anselm was inspired by a spirit of prophecy in these incidents, the plain facts of the case show what is to be believed," Eadmer writes.

On a trip to Cluny, a crowd surrounding a frenzied madwoman besieged Anselm, pleading that he heal her. Anselm was horrified, and "feeling that he would not escape on any other terms, gave way to them to this extent," making the sign of the cross, Eadmer reports. "When he had done this, they let go his reins and he rode quickly away. He pulled his cowl over his head, drew away from his companions, and rode on alone, being moved by pity and bewailing most tenderly the sad plight of the unhappy woman." News reached them at Cluny that she was healed. During a thunderstorm at another monastery, a great bolt of lightning struck the hay house, scattering monks and setting the house on fire. Anselm quoted a proverb about a neighbor's burning house, hurried outside, and gave the sign of the cross. "Instantly you might have seen the flames sinking down as if they were stooping to receive his blessing," Eadmer testified.

As abbot of Bec, Anselm was charged with reviewing the monastery properties, many of which were across the English Channel—land, church buildings, and estates that the wealthy faithful had given as tithes. Anselm's travels over the next decade—three trips to England in all—didn't undermine his literary projects. He was as prolific as ever, and began to seriously collect his letters, prayers, and meditations.

With God's existence proved, Anselm moved into other stormy scholastic territory. In the 1080s, he produced three theological works: *On Truth*, *On Free Will*, and *On the Fall of the Devil*. Knowledge, freedom, and why evil exists—Anselm never failed to pick the big ones. They were called his "three treatises." As he wrote in wax, his scribes copied his text onto the finest parchment. They produced multiple copies, pressed and bound them, for Anselm's writings had become bankable. They could be sold to libraries or circulated to the right people, such as barons and baronesses, the patrons of the day.

As tends to happen with prolific scholars, however, Anselm opened himself up to the critics. The "schools"—as the centers of scholastic professionals were to be called—started producing more heretics: monks and scholars who veered away from orthodoxy. One of the most famous heretics of Anselm's day was Roscelin of Compiegne, nicknamed the "composer of a strange new song" for having presented one of the earliest arguments for "nominalism," the idea that essences

are just names (*nomina*) and not realities, contrary to
Anselm's philosophy. Anselm might have avoided a
squabble with Roscelin, who was popular with students
in another region of France, had Roscelin not quoted
Anselm to support his heresies. "I began to compose a
letter against this error," recalls Anselm of an aborted
plan to defend himself to the local bishop. The letter
provides one of the few surviving accounts of Roscelin.
It also led to a four-year project, a doctrinal manifesto
that paused for a few sentences to condemn what others were calling the "nominalist sect." Although Anselm
does not name Roscelin, he laments "those contemporary logicians (rather, the heretical logicians) who consider universal essences to be merely vocal emanations."

This surprise encounter with Roscelin's nominalism was Anselm's first theological war, and he came
away the wiser. Now he wrote not only to persuade, but
to defend himself from rumors and hearsay.

WHILE Anselm scribbled in his dank cell, the fate of
England was being decided. William the Conqueror
died in 1087, probably of a heart attack brought on
by his legendary girth. (His body burst when it was
forced into the stone sarcophagus.) The next day his
son took the throne. He was known as William the
Younger, William II; alternatively, for his fiery red hair,
Rufus. Nineteen months later Lanfranc died, and the
archbishopric of Canterbury was empty. Here Rufus
showed his cunning. He left the archbishopric vacant

for the next four years and helped himself to its revenues. He needed the money: after the succession, his armies were busy securing the frontiers, for there were still rivals in Wales and Scotland, and Vikings always on the lookout for an opportune moment to invade. Furthermore, Rufus wanted to conquer Normandy.

Happily ignorant of such intrigues, Anselm packed his bags for a fourth trip to England. He was fifty-nine years old. He needed to review his Bec properties, meet Rufus, and answer the spiritual plea of supporters in Chester, a city on the west coast. In September 1092, Anselm and his small party of monks crossed the channel, landing at the white cliffs of Dover, and made their way to London, heading for Westminster Palace.

As Anselm entered, the king rose from his throne, as Eadmer described the scene, and greeted Anselm at the door "with joy." He fell upon Anselm's neck and led him by the hand to the throne room. After a few pleasantries, Anselm took the king aside and scolded him for the reports of sexual excess in his court. Other chroniclers of the time confirmed Anselm's charge: Rufus "used concubines and because of that died without an heir," according to the era's Welsh-written *Chronicle of Princes*. Anselm was also concerned about sodomy.

The visit was brief, and Anselm headed for Westminster Abbey, where his former student at Bec, the monk Gilbert Crispin, had risen to become prior. It was a welcome respite. Anselm worked on collecting his letters. Over the years, he had developed firm views about how monks and nuns should behave. As he once said, "No one, after he has become dead to the world and has entered the cloister, ought on any account, even in intention, return to worldly affairs." This went for nuns, too, as two episodes involving runaway nuns made clear. Both were from royal families. The first was Matilda, daughter of the king of Scotland. The king had put her in a nunnery to get an education before she married. Anselm viewed her as having taken vows. When she left, Anselm demanded that the local bishop get her back. Eventually, a church council sided with Matilda. (Seven years later, Anselm, who could turn on a dime, would preside at the wedding that made her Queen of England.)

The other case was Gunhilda, surviving daughter of King Harold, killed at the Battle of Hastings in 1066. Like Matilda, Gunhilda lived at the Wilton Abbey nunnery, southwest of London, but didn't lack for suitors, one of whom, Count Alan Rufus, managed to spirit her away. In early 1093, she left Wilton Abbey to be his mistress or wife.

At first blush, Anselm seemed offended that she had abandoned her vows, which she maintained she'd never taken: she'd only worn the veil. When Alan Rufus died later that year, Gunhilda married his brother. Eventually she returned to Wilton Abbey and died there, famous for her monastic piety. But in the heat of the passions of 1093, Anselm had written her two letters. The first had the tone of a love letter: "You once said that you wished to be ever with me so that you could enjoy an uninterrupted talk." The second was in chilling contrast: Anselm was obviously resentful that Gunhilda had chosen the elusive pleasures of the world:

> You loved Count Alan Rufus, and he you. Where is he now? What has become of the lover whom you loved? Go now and lie with him in the bed where he now lies; gather his worms into your bosom; embrace his corpse; kiss his bare teeth from which the flesh has fallen. He does not now care for your love in which he delighted while he lived; and the flesh which you desired now rots.

Anselm may have been a monk in love, but he tended to express himself with a passion that was hard to decipher—was it earthly or ethereal?

In any event, his letters to Gunhilda were the last of a personal, intimate nature. From then on, he was all business.

CHAPTER 3

Canterbury Tales

IN the spring of 1093, Anselm was staying with Crispin at Westminster, still trying to figure out how to meet the king. He needed the regime's blessing on the properties, a symbolic matter known in the Middle Ages as "homage." For six months Rufus had made him cool his heels. Then the king moved his court to Gloucester and the Royal Hunting Forest. Jockeying for position, Anselm moved to lodgings nearby. But when a breathless messenger finally showed up at his door, the news he brought was unexpected—and not good. The king was dying. He needed a priest.

At the court, a cluster of stone buildings and a church set in a dense woodland, Anselm was led to the king's bedside. From what can be gathered, Anselm first heard a bedside confession and applied the last rites. Eadmer gives a general account of the events, but much is left to the imagination.

However it happened, Anselm made the dying king focus on a few church matters he had neglected. For one thing, he had failed to confirm the Bec church properties, nor had he provided his people with a spiritual shepherd, leaving the archbishopric of Canterbury vacant for four years. There is no indication that

Anselm was dropping his own name for the post, but again, he was a man torn. He despised administrative jobs, but he could still hear the old French archbishop, Maurilius, reminding him: "If you are ever called to a higher office you are by no means to decline it."

What happened next, recounted by a stunned Eadmer, requires the imagination of a Hollywood set director to picture in detail. The king is on his bed. The royal principals crowd around. Rufus grabs Anselm's hand. He tries to press the archbishop's staff, or crosier, into Anselm's reluctant fingers, but Anselm resists. The bishops move in. They pry open Anselm's fist and put the staff in it, reducing him to tears. At that moment the king declares him archbishop. As Eadmer recounts, "When Anselm heard this, he wore himself almost to death in his objections, and in resisting and fighting against it." But the gathering prevailed. "He was seized, and forcibly carried rather than led into the neighboring church with hymns and rejoicings."

It was a highly unusual succession. Anselm had just had the crosier forced into his hand by "lay investiture," or secular authority. Lay investiture was to become the last great dispute of his life, and an issue that rocked Europe's throne rooms for another generation. The question was this: Who ruled the spiritual domain, the king or the pope?

In the end, the king didn't die, turning the bedside tragedy into a comedy; his stubborn will to survive would alter Anselm's destiny. Anselm accepted his fate by "obedience and necessity," Eadmer tells us, and received approval from the duke of Normandy and the archbishop of Rouen. He returned his abbot's staff to Bec and in September arrived at the royal court in Winchester to pay "homage" to Rufus, a bow-and-scrape ceremony full of symbolic trappings.

On September 25, 1093, Anselm was installed upon the Canterbury throne, and in early December he was consecrated by the other senior church figure in England, the archbishop of York. But Anselm's real superior—or rival—in England was the king. Now he had to deal with Rufus toe-to-toe. Their bickering seemed endless. It began a few months after Anselm became archbishop, when he attended the king's Christmas court at Gloucester. At first all was harmonious. But there was one sticking point: Anselm was supposed to pay the king a thousand pounds for the archbishop's job—the dread simony that infuriated Cluniac reformers. Ever diplomatic, Eadmer called Rufus's demand the "thank-offering for his munificence." Anselm refused. He had been invested and had paid homage, but even Anselm knew that bribe money, extracted from his hard-working monasteries, was a violation of God's will.

Yet kings and archbishops had to get along, or else exile or kill one another. That the world was so corrupt didn't surprise Anselm: it was the very doctrine of his faith. In effect, Anselm compartmentalized. He spent his life defending the church and the soul, but let the world go its own way. He wasn't interested in the military crusades decreed by the pope, but, ever a pragmatist, supported his corrupt, red-haired king in matters of military defense. Once enthroned, Anselm was an English nationalist. He saved his battles for church rights.

In early 1094, the king had gathered his court and army at Hastings, near the English coast. Rufus wanted to take the fight to Normandy, the domain of his chief rival, his older brother Robert, Duke of Normandy. Rufus waited for a good wind, but the channel was whipped with fog and turbulence, stalling his attack until March. The king had already summoned Anselm to give an expeditionary blessing to this sibling rivalry. Now Anselm was stuck in the bad weather as well. The collective leadership of England, including its archbishop, stood in the cold fog with nothing to do.

Anselm was at wits' end. He decided to confront the king again about calling a church council. Churches were crumbling, church law was ignored, morals were lax. The solution, as always, was to call a meeting. Rufus still wanted his "thank-offering." Anselm replied that the king must finally recognize the pope, Urban II. Otherwise, Rome would not deliver to Anselm the symbolic object of his authority, the wool pallium worn over an archbishop's shoulders. "The king listened to all this with the greatest displeasure," writes Eadmer, "and declared that he would do nothing about any of these things to please him."

The conflict between Rufus and Anselm had reached the boiling point. In early 1095, Rufus tried to usurp Anselm by calling his own Council at Rockingham. But political reality brought the king to his senses. He could not conceivably conquer Normandy, uniting it with England, if he had the archbishop and pope as enemies. In a strange twist of history, it was Pope Urban II who helped the recalcitrant Rufus solve the problem. In 1095, Urban launched the First Crusade; one of its first enthusiasts was Robert, the king's brother, who headed off for glory in Jerusalem. He and Rufus delayed their sibling showdown, with all its political complexities, for a few more years. Now the wiser, however, Rufus sent a messenger to Rome recognizing Urban II. Soon after, a papal legate arrived in England with the pallium. On May 27, 1095, the final symbol of his authority was draped on Anselm's aging shoulders.

As might be expected, Anselm was more irritable than ever. "As a bishop he ought to have gone on to better things; but he saw his days and nights taken up with secular business," Eadmer observes. "The king's mind was worked up into a fury against him." Anselm longed to get back to his tranquil monastery, likening himself to an owl at peace with her brood. In Rufus's world, he mused to his friends, the owl was "attacked and torn to pieces when she is among crows and rooks and other birds, and everything then is far from well with her; so it is with me." Indeed, he would often "tremble with horror" at how the secular world might destroy his soul.

Four years into his archbishopric, he still hadn't been able to hold a church council. Rufus kept putting it off. Anselm had played the loyal part, supervising a defense rampart on the southern coast while Rufus warred on his kingdom's northern boundary. Later, in the summer of 1097, when the king's campaign had gone well in Wales, Anselm hoped he'd return in a generous mood and hold the council. But the king had only bitter complaints: the monasteries had sent him poor-caliber soldiers, hardly the knights he needed. Anselm had had enough. Ever loyal, he asked the king for permission to visit the pope in Rome. At first, the king refused, but he finally acquiesced in October 1097. Thus did Anselm begin his first exile.

It was October 25 when Anselm gathered the monks of Canterbury to announce his exile and urge them to stay in the monastic profession. "The long drawn-out dispute between our lord king and myself about the reform of Christian discipline has at last come to this," he said. He went willingly in hopes that "my journey will be of some use to the *liberty of the church*"—his first public use of that politically charged phrase. "But the hour forbids more talk." The monks were in tears as Anselm walked across the grounds to the church, took the pilgrim's staff from the altar, and headed to the coast. The wind was so long in coming that he almost turned back. In November the sails suddenly filled, and Anselm crossed the channel, landing at Wissan on the northern coast of France.

Leaving England must have been a great relief. It solved nothing for Canterbury, however, for the king was once again siphoning off the revenues of bishoprics and abbeys. Anselm went to see his old friends in Lyon and promptly wrote to Pope Urban II, asking for permission to resign his post as archbishop of Canterbury. But there was no way out. Instead, the pope invited Anselm to Rome—and in the next twelve months dragged him into theological battle.

It all began one April day in 1098. Anselm arrived from the north, reaching Saint Peter's Basilica in its ancient location on the Tiber River. He and Eadmer approached the basilica, entering one of its five front doorways, and reached a front atrium, called the Garden of Paradise, adorned as it was with glittering mosaics, chandeliers, statues, and tombs. The wood-beamed basilica was shaped like a giant cross and stretched the length of a football field. When Anselm was led to the papal chamber to meet the aging Urban II, he bowed and kissed the pope. The assembly applauded as he took a seat. God's warrior, a humble confronter of kings, had arrived. The pope proceeded to lay it on fairly thick (he was not about to accept Anselm's resignation). "We consider him as a master steeped in all branches of the liberal arts," Urban declared, "[an] apostolic patriarch of that other world" (England), and yet "so excellent a humility and constancy rules his mind." Undeterred by the "perils of the sea or by the vast expanses of foreign soil," Anselm

had come to ask papal advice, when it was the papacy
"who rather need[s] his counsel."

Urban was no aristocrat or recluse. A Frenchman,
he was former prior at Cluny, a papal diplomat, and
still a Cluniac—that is, an advocate of a strong papacy.
Now, Anselm was to be a part of that strengthening
of the Latin pontiff. The first task, later that summer,
would send Anselm to the Council of Bari on the east
coast of Italy, where he was to try to persuade the Greek
Church to accept the Latin theology on the Holy Spirit.
Anselm's defense of the Trinity, *De Incarnatione Verbi*
(which had been written against Roscelin, the nominalist), had impressed Urban. At Bari, Anselm exhorted
the Greek theologians that the Holy Spirit proceeded
from the Father "and the Son," as was clearly indicated
by the Latin word *filioque* (from *filius*, meaning "son,"
and *que*, meaning "and"). For the Greeks, it was more
obvious that the Holy Spirit proceeded from the Father
through the Son.

Anselm tried his best, but to no avail. The failure
of Urban to persuade the Greeks, even after launching a
goodwill crusade to help Byzantium fight the Muslims,
was a show of papal weakness noticed with some satisfaction by the secular courts of France, England,
Germany, Spain, and Sicily. But Urban had one more
card up his sleeve, and he would produce it the next
April when the great Easter Council convened in Rome.
Anselm, who had wintered in the Italian hillsides, was
invited back to Rome: perhaps more than his bout with

the Greeks, the Easter Council would shape the next stage of his career. It was April 1099, and as the assembled clerics struggled to hear the debates and council decrees above the noise of pilgrims and tourists in the great basilica, at least one announcement rang clear to Anselm. The pope declared that never again (after twenty years of slippage) would a secular leader "invest," that is, appoint, a clergyman to a church office.

The condemnation of 1099 was the toughest stand taken so far in the growing investiture controversy, which many historians today see as the major political issue of that era. The clash erupted in every country and wasn't finally resolved until 1122, well after Anselm's death. As always, the church and the state blunted each other's authority with a compromise. Under the 1122 Concordat of Worms, kings would not invest high church officials, but these ecclesiastics would still have to pay due homage. In truth, it was all about symbolic objects and acts—the ceremonial exchange of staffs, rings, scepters, bows, blessings, crowns, and official seals. The symbols made peace and soothed egos, so they were all for the good.

After the Easter Council of 1099, Anselm was persuaded to take a hard line against the king of England. In this action, he was deeply influenced by his other great friend, the intractable Hugh of Lyons, an old-guard figure who was the Gregorian reform movement's chief legate in Normandy. Hugh had long tried to bring clergy and princes into line. He urged Anselm, who was staying with him at the time, to do the same. Anselm wasn't a political thinker at all. His view was religious: he owed obedience to a *papal* decree. And as would be seen, if the next pope wavered, Anselm owed obedience to God, even in defiance of papal compromises.

A new battle cry burst from the lips of Hugh and Anselm: *Libertas Ecclesiae,* or "the liberty of the church." It was an important movement, asserted in all church institutions at the end of the eleventh century; the idea of a self-governing corporation would serve as a basis for a new institution, the university. Anselm stayed in France, based mostly in Lyons, another sixteen months—long enough to witness two major deaths and a shift in European politics. Later in 1099, Urban II passed from the scene, and Pope Paschal II was elected to take over. A few weeks after that, Rufus was killed— an August 2nd hunting "accident," as it was delicately phrased. The scene was New Forest, a dense, dark, and mysterious place. Less mysteriously, Rufus's younger brother, Henry, was also in the woods that day. Henry quickly rode to Winchester and seized the treasury. In London three days later, King Henry I was crowned by the archbishop of York, a cleric softened up by the new king's lavish promises of church benefits and freedoms.

In August 1100, having sized up his power base, Henry invited Anselm back to England. Anselm hit the shores of Dover on September 23 and met Henry a few days later at Salisbury. Until then, Anselm had never mentioned politics in his letters. But a new spirit had superseded his former otherworldliness. Guiltily, he admitted that "the king gave me the archbishopric," a clear assault on "the liberty of the church." At Salisbury, Anselm drew a line. He and Henry clashed from the start. Henry demanded that Anselm pay him homage as a condition to gain back church properties. He also wanted Anselm to consecrate some bishops chosen by the king. Anselm's obedience lay elsewhere.

Henry played for time, letting Anselm have his way while he sent a messenger to Rome for clarification. Now Anselm was caught between two very hard places, a king and a pope. Henry was a secular manipulator in the great English tradition, while the new pope, Paschal II, was of necessity backing off from Urban's tough decrees. During his nineteen-year pontificate, Paschal undid the Gregorian juggernaut, which had boosted papal power by browbeating secular leaders. Those leaders always had military and political threats in reserve, such as invasions or property confiscations, so Paschal was forced to make deals with the royals of Europe, which left Anselm pretty much on his own in dealing with King Henry. Fortunately for Anselm, Henry was still politically weak in England, where he paid nobles and churchmen to support him against Robert, the Duke of Normandy. Robert was back from the Crusades, bolder than ever. He was preparing to invade England to seize the throne.

King Henry needed Anselm as an ally, and they settled into a working relationship. By November, Anselm

was presiding at Henry's marriage to Matilda, the supposed former nun. Soon enough, a national war would
tighten their alliance. The military crisis exploded in
summer 1101, when Robert breached the coastline, with
all the thunder and rattle of wooden ships, knights in
armor, and the clatter of horse hooves and marching
lines of Norman shields. Anselm had always been a
nationalist. Henry was a pragmatist: he quickly declared
loyalty to the pope, rallying his kingdom and repulsing
his brother's advance. Robert pulled back to Normandy,
not knowing that the worst was still to come.

Long after the battle, Rome finally sent a letter
of clarification to the king of England that included
a strict decree against investiture and homage. But it
was as ambiguous as possible about what was required.
From his position of strength, King Henry demanded
that Anselm give him what he had wanted since
the beginning—a payment for his office—or leave
England. For the next six months, Anselm withdrew to
his monastic estates, engaged in a battle of wills. From
his position of weakness in Rome, Paschal insisted that
Henry recognize the liberty of the church. This was the
high point of the "investiture controversy" in England.
Rome and London had hardened their positions, and
Anselm was pitifully pressed in between. Left in the
lurch, he packed for his "second exile," crossing the
channel on April 7, 1103.

At a leisurely pace, Anselm, accompanied as always
by his dutiful biographer, Eadmer, headed for central

France, the former haunt of Gaunilo (defender of "the fool"), to see an old friend, Ivo, now bishop of Chartres. When Anselm arrived, he found a Romanesque stone-and-wood cathedral—for once not burnt to the ground. A half century after Ivo, another bishop began to erect the soaring Gothic cathedral of later fame on its foundations. Anselm and Eadmer then turned north to Bec. They waited for cooler weather, and in mid-August headed for Rome. It was on this trip that they carried a special package, the thick manuscript of Anselm's *Prayers* and *Meditations* to be delivered to Countess Matilda in Tuscany.

When Anselm arrived in Rome in October, he found King Henry's envoy already there. His session with the pope was inconclusive. Anselm could see that the Curia took Henry's side. After all, England was at stake. Anselm's confusion only deepened. On the way back to England, he crossed paths with the king's envoy. They compared letters, and Anselm could see that he was in trouble. The Curia had sent two letters to Henry. One gave him royal prerogative; the other sided with Anselm, defending his concerns for the "liberty of the church," with regard to properties and appointments. Clearly, the king would follow the first option, the envoy said. He warned Anselm not to come back unless he planned to restore the customs of the Rufus era. Anselm had only one resort. He detoured to Lyons and began procedures to excommunicate the soul of King Henry from the church, casting it into utter oblivion.

If Anselm desired to escape the headaches of
Canterbury, this drawn-out process was his chance.
He had to write three letters demanding repentance
before excommunication could occur. This, too, stalled
Anselm—to his advantage. He lingered in France for a year
and a half, up to the spring of 1105. In England, Henry was
feeling the pressure. The old sibling rivalry had not died:
Henry was about to invade Normandy and imprison
his brother Robert. The last thing Henry needed was an
excommunication on his head. Diplomacy was best, he
decided. He sent his sister to Normandy to arrange a July
meeting in L'Aigle with Anselm.

The excommunication had been prompted by
Henry's seizure of church properties, and at the meeting, Henry promised to return the church properties
he had seized. But he also insisted that he had as much
right as Rufus to invest churchmen and demand homage. Emboldened by the spirit of 1099—the investiture
decree at the Easter Council—Anselm said 'no.' The
negotiations were off, and Anselm headed to Bec. Over
his head, a compromise was reached between Rome
and England. The king could receive homage, but not
invest. As far as Anselm was concerned, this was back-
pedaling, but when the papal letter of explanation
reached him in April 1106, he was ready to go home. He
was ensconced at Canterbury by September. He had a
year and a half left to live, and he was happy to lounge
on his archbishop's throne, for once in peace, holding
his staff and wearing his pallium on high occasions.

In January 1109, he took to his sick bed at Canterbury. For all his struggles, Anselm had not found a great political solution. His heart had been in his proof of God and in his writings. He grew weaker in April, and Eadmer reports that he had turned his attention to the origin of the soul, a theological problem that would be hard to solve after death. At Mass, friends read to Anselm from the Passion, the story of Christ's last days. Anselm was near the end. The monks put him on a cot of sackcloth and ashes. He died as dawn broke on April 29, 1109. That same day, Abbot Hugh, the powerful leader of Cluny, also departed this world. As one historian recounts, the coincidence "was frequently remarked on by contemporaries."

THE so-called "investiture controversies" of the period played out differently in different countries. When the German emperor Henry, for example, arrived in Rome to be crowned by Paschal, they got in a dispute over money, and the emperor threw the pope in prison. England and France worked out a far more peaceful and classic arrangement: kings received homage, but only the church appointed clergy and bishops.

Back when Paschal had double-crossed Anselm to do business with King Henry, the pope might have felt guilty. What else could explain a gift he gave to Anselm: he allowed Canterbury to be viewed as the No. 1 bishopric in England, an ecclesiastical status in each nation called "primacy." York had to take second rank. The pri-

macy of Canterbury is Anselm's only practical legacy.
Unlike other churchmen, the lawyer popes and bishops
of the future, Anselm gave great weight to local custom,
and in this he saw Canterbury as autonomous, despite
the growing power of the papal system.

He had fought two kings, not out of a clear political theory of church and state, but out of a sense of
obedience to the church doctrine of liberty, both of the
will and of the institution. It would take another archbishop, Thomas à Becket, for Canterbury to assert an
absolute physical resistance to an English monarch. On
Canterbury's altar steps, Thomas was assassinated by
the monarch's minions for his cry of *libertas ecclesiae*.

During his tenure, Anselm was always a shadowy
figure at Canterbury. If his following was narrow, it was
a product of the closed monastic common life. That
life differed greatly from the secular schools, where students came and went. They latched onto masters and
became disciples. The masters were the axis of a "school
of thought," which moved with them between institutions. Anselm wrote the *Proslogion* and *Monologion*, his
most distinctive works, in virtual isolation. Yet in his
lifetime both texts were studied in Lyons and known
of in Rome.

The committed atheist of the eleventh century
would have been a rare figure, or certainly a circum-
spect one. Neither Anselm nor Eadmer offered a helpful profile—though they both elicited countless stories
of human wickedness. Anselm's atheist was the figure in

the Bible, the "fool" who said there is no God. Anselm had no principled atheist in the medieval landscape to persuade with the two arguments of his *Proslogion*. He aimed at believers who, undeveloped as thinkers, might find the joys of discovering God in the mind. He wanted to use the joys of logic to deepen their experience. He wanted to prove that God's existence is a necessary part of human thinking.

Born into the eleventh century, Anselm stood between Augustine and Thomas Aquinas, the two salutary figures of Western philosophy. But Anselm was in a different situation from both. Augustine and Aquinas lived and worked in a world that was not uniformly Christian. Both had long philosophical traditions to draw upon and used philosophy to persuade a secular world of Christian truths. By comparison, Anselm faced no such challenge. He worked in an insular community with simple traditions. His main resource and novelty was a process invented in his own mind, and revealed in his own literary style.

Anselm was a type of modern, as he warned his readers. He took words seriously. He gave them a supernatural power that would seem strange to us today. But however he used them, he analyzed them with the rigor of a modern grammarian. Like a mathematician, he created his own premises and constructed a model of knowledge that was at least as sound as Aristotle's logic, and more sophisticated than any logic that the great Augustine had devised.

The Benedictine order held a monopoly in Europe, peaking in 1050, but it was the source of new ideas as well. The growing wealth of the monasteries piqued enough monk consciences for them to call for a return to simplicity and even sacrifice. Over the next century, the Benedictines gave rise to their revolutionary offspring, the Augustinians and Cistercians. Both were austere, but the Cistercians organized with almost military rigor, building vast commercial complexes on the frontier—the first international corporations. By the thirteenth century, Europe's growing population and wealth produced the first great cities, and these became a magnet, first for the Augustinians, and ultimately for their successors, the Dominicans and Franciscans, the urban "friars" who would dominate the future of Europe.

These rebellions would have been unimaginable to Anselm. He had no problem with well-heeled monasteries, as long as monks lived in pious obedience. Corrupt kings? Not a big deal, as long as they let the church alone. But if Anselm seemed politically conservative and culturally old-fashioned, he was also strikingly modern in his consciousness of himself as an individual—what we would call his sense of identity. The Anselmian mind professed humility while presuming to understand God.

CHAPTER 4

The Friars of Oxford

A NSELM'S proof of God did not have a large audience in the century after his death, although his biography, thanks to Eadmer, gained a wide circulation. The Ontological Argument in the *Proslogion* did not transfix European minds until the great universities of Europe matured and produced the great theological scholastics: in particular, Thomas Aquinas. That peak came in the thirteenth century, more than a hundred years after Anselm was entombed at Canterbury.

Anselm had been part of this first phase, built upon just a few remnants of Aristotle's logic. He had used Aristotle's two simplest tools: the syllogism and the argument of what was possible and impossible. Armed with these, he had developed a proof of God "in the mind"—what philosophers later called an a priori argument. But while Anselm wandered France, the Crusaders of Latin Christianity made a revolutionary discovery in Spain. There, in Toledo, they found the lost works of Aristotle. Their translation took a hundred more years, but as they came to light, the rest of Aristotle's works inspired another kind of proof for God: a proof, based on Aristotle's physics, from the "effects" in the world back to the cause. Modern philosophers called this an *a posteriori* argument.

When the Crusaders invaded Spain, it was viewed as the "reconquest" of land taken by the Muslims. The crown jewel was the taking of Toledo in 1085. About the time Anselm died, the new Christian rulers were just beginning to realize the significance of what they had found in Toledo's storehouses, as well as storehouses in Sicily. It was nearly Aristotle's entire corpus, but translated into Arabic and Syriac from the original Greek. It was a development that would transform the intellectual life of Europe.

The work of translation began in Toledo, where Jewish, Christian, and Muslim scholars gathered in great library rooms, surrounded by Moorish architecture and dripping fountains, reading the text aloud. Between 1125 and 1152, Archbishop Raimundo ruled in Toledo, where he summoned these teams of international scholars and scribes, among whom Gerard of Cremona emerged as a virtuoso, translating about seventy works, mostly from Arabic into Latin.

Once it was in full view, the philosophy of Aristotle provided Christianity with a system to describe the cosmos and a method of analysis. For Aristotle, the power of all life was motion, so he conceived God as the first motion, or "prime mover," the ultimate cause of activity in an eternal material universe. After God and motion, reason was next in greatness, a virtue that made human beings superior among creatures. Intelligence was their highest pursuit: "Intellect more than anything *is* man." To increase knowledge, Aristotle invented logic, maintaining—not entirely without justification—that before he introduced his method, "[n]othing existed at all." The method was analytical, defining the nature of things, their relations, and their contradictions. "It is not possible to untie a knot which one does not know," he wrote in his *Metaphysics*. "Therefore we should have surveyed all the difficulties beforehand."

Between 1200 and 1650, Aristotle's framework dominated liberal arts education. But it was not the only organizing principle in medieval learning, for even before the high tide of Greek translations arrived, medieval scholars had invented a new vehicle of knowledge: the textbook. It appeared around the time of the capture of Toledo. Referred to as a book of "sentences"—or collection of opinions—the textbook became the fulcrum of university study. It was a lack of textbooks in Anselm's day that explains why his work didn't circulate in Europe until a century after his death.

Writing a textbook was a way to fame. Its inventor was the Italian scholar Peter Lombard. Around 1158, Peter compiled what was known for generations afterward as Lombard's *Four Books of Sentences*. The books listed all the questions that tormented Christian thinkers, and offered a parade of speculative answers culled from ancient philosophers, Muslim and Jewish scholars, church fathers, and contemporary writers. Any serious university student in thirteenth-century Europe had to master either Aristotle or Lombard's *Sentences* before going on to medicine, law, or theology.

This confluence of textbooks and universities took place in the novel setting of a city, where new ideas were readily transmitted by a transient population. The university had eclipsed the bishop's school. The first real university appeared in Paris about 1170. It set the pattern of a corporation, a group of constituents that claimed legal rights in relation to the church, king, and city fathers. The creation of a university usually began with a "master," or scholar, who in turn served as a magnet for other teachers in arts, theology, medicine, and law, and students from all over Europe who formed nationalist fraternities when they arrived.

Fifty years after the University of Paris was organized, a new feature arose in university towns: the growing presence of Dominican and Franciscan friars, who migrated there to set up religious communities and missions.

The founder of the Dominicans was Dominic de Guzman, a monk from Spain. In 1206, Dominic traveled with a bishop through Montpelier, on the southern coast of France, a region known for its heretical movements, and was appalled by the failure of the upper-class bishops to persuade the masses back to orthodoxy. To reach ordinary people, these "Dominicans" styled themselves as lowly heresy-fighters, preachers who lived off charity and moved among the common folk. Dominic held the inaugural meeting of his followers in

Toulouse in 1217. By the time of his death in 1221, the Order of Preachers, as they came to be known, had divided up among them the major cities of Europe—most notably Paris, where the order flourished.

As Dominic was beginning to make his name, Francis of Assisi, the son of a wealthy merchant family in Italy, listened to a life-changing sermon about the poverty and humility of Christ and his followers. It was 1209, and after the sermon, the twenty-eight-year-old Francis, in a cathartic moment, renounced worldly things to devote himself to the works of God. He led a group of eleven followers to Rome, where he was rebuffed by a busy papal court. But Francis was dogged. He saw the three main religious movements that preceded him—the Benedictines, Cistercians, and Augustinians—as worldly bureaucracies, and proposed instead a movement of voluntary poverty. Christ and his apostles, the new doctrine held, "owned" nothing.

Now face to face, the Dominicans and Franciscans lived and learned from each other as their itinerant forces crossed paths, especially in the cities. They both centralized. The Franciscans followed the Dominicans to the universities. The Dominicans borrowed Franciscan proletarian styles. While Dominic pioneered the well-oiled campaign, the Franciscans always seemed on the verge of anarchy—which explained why the papacy ultimately tapped the Dominicans to lead the Inquisition. Even so, the Franciscans, with their proletariat base, generated twice the membership, with 28,000 friars at their medieval peak.

Ultimately, camaraderie developed between friars and students, who were both drawn to the universities. Students who lacked jobs after graduation often joined the friars, finding financial support, social acceptance, and a chance to pursue their studies. Friardom offered support for a lifetime of study and teaching. On occasion, a renowned secular scholar converted, helping to found a Franciscan or Dominican "chair" or "house." The classic example is Alexander of Hales, a teacher at the University of Paris.

When Alexander became a Franciscan in 1231, he was the order's first university teacher of theology. He was also a great promoter of Anselm's Ontological Proof of God. In addition to Alexander, fourteen other medieval thinkers, beginning in the age of the university, took up the topic of Anselm's proof, and nine of them declared it valid. One who did not, however, was Thomas Aquinas.

AQUINAS, born in his aristocratic parents' castle just outside Aquino, central Italy, was destined to reflect the temperament of his German father and Norman mother, who promptly enrolled him as a child monk at the mountaintop monastery of Monte Cassino. When the pope and German emperor started warring nearby in 1239, they moved Thomas, then age fourteen, to the "studium generale," or university, recently founded by the German emperor in Naples, a peaceful haven.

By his young adulthood, Aquinas was a tall, quiet, and heavyset *wunderkind*, though one unsuspecting teacher called him a "dumb ox." After joining the Dominicans, he was sent to Paris in 1245 to study under the science-oriented theologian Albert, later "Albert the Great" as a bishop and head of the German Dominicans. By then the university, set amid a bustling city on the Seine with brawling students and entrepreneurial scholars in gowns and birettas, was about ninety years old. The campus was clustered around Notre Dame Cathedral on the Left Bank, where masters and students met for lessons in cloisters and rented rooms. The Latin Quarter was the center, so named because only the Latin language was allowed to be spoken there. Students were organized by nationalities, and "colleges" formed; the friars had their own houses, teachers, and students.

Loyal to his teacher Albert, Aquinas followed him to Cologne but returned to Paris in 1252 to teach on the Dominican faculty, which meant lecturing on Lombard's *Sentences*. He soon began work on his own version of the book, as his master Albert had done. He completed his commentary on the "four books" around 1256. Eventually, as word spread of Aquinas's talents, the Dominican superiors summoned him south around 1259 to live at the Dominican monastery in Orvieto, north of Rome on the Tiber River—a two-

day journey of about seventy miles. There he prepared
new members of the order for their mission work. The
pope also lived in Orvieto at the time. But the most significant meeting was between Aquinas, who moved in
Dominican circles in Italy, and William of Moerbeke,
the Flemish archbishop of Corinth. Moerbeke, a fellow Dominican, was translating Aristotle's works into
Latin; he would complete fifty in his lifetime. While
Moerbeke translated, Aquinas read.

Aquinas referred to Aristotle simply as "The
Philosopher." Was there any other? By 1265, when the
Dominicans gave Aquinas the mission of establishing
a house of studies in Rome, he had begun writing his
Summa Theologica, and Aristotle was its central pagan
character. Following Aristotle, Aquinas argued that all
knowledge came by the senses (*a posteriori* knowledge).
Therefore, human beings could know God only by anal-
ogy with the world, such as the relationship between
parents and children, or the observation of cause and
effect. Aquinas also cited Anselm's argument—that the
very thought of God proves God's existence—without mentioning him by name. Aquinas, like Gaunilo,
seemed to be more sympathetic to the fool than to
Anselm's proof. He writes:

> Yet, granted, that everyone understands that by
> this name God is signified something than which
> nothing greater can be thought, nevertheless, it does
> not therefore follow that he understands that what

the name signifies exists actually, but only that it exists mentally. Nor can it be argued that it actually exists, unless it be admitted that there actually exists something than which nothing greater can be thought; and this precisely is not admitted by those who hold that God does not exist.

But Aquinas refused to give up on the demonstration of God's existence. He offered five ways that God could be known by his "effects" in the world:

1. Motion suggests a first mover.
2. Causes suggest a first cause.
3. The contingency of things suggests a necessary source.
4. The world's gradations of less and more require an ultimate standard.
5. Natural things have purposeful ends, so there must be an intelligent governor.

Aquinas's rejection of Anselm had major historical consequences. He sharpened the medieval debate on whether God was known only by effects or directly in the mind. "We can demonstrate the existence of God from His effects," Aquinas asserted, "though from them we cannot know God perfectly as He is in His essence." Aquinas's verdict on "proofs" in general was stated at the front of the *Summa*. For generations afterward, the *Summa*'s description of the Anselmian argument was better known than Anselm's own words in the *Proslogion*. Aquinas perpetuated the Aristotelian tradition, while Anselm's work lagged behind, mired in the more primitive notions of divine illumination inherited from Plato and Augustine.

While trying to complete the *Summa*, Aquinas received another assignment. In 1269 he was sent back to Paris to battle with rival secular scholars. They had begun to adopt a new interpretation of Aristotle offered by Averroes, the Arab commentator, whose works were among those found in Toledo and Sicily. Averroes advanced the Greek idea that the material universe had no beginning, and was thus eternal and uncreated. It was an obvious philosophical problem for the Christian doctrine of the Creation *ex nihilo*, or "out of nothing." Averroes also denied that a person's soul survived as an individual being after death, but rather merged into a collective soul that contained all of humanity.

Aquinas was put in charge of a new Dominican house of studies, which became renowned in Paris for its erudition. His delicate task was to take back "The Philosopher" and his metaphysics from Averroes's advocates. It was no easy task in a city of perpetual contention, fueled by French nationalism that resented papal or Italian interventions. Aquinas's work in Paris might have consumed his last years had it not been for the intervention of the king of Naples. In 1272, the king invited him to return to Naples to reorganize the university where he had begun his studies. Two years later, summoned to a church council in Lyons, France, Aquinas traveled by mule, but fell ill between Naples and Rome. He died in bed at a Cistercian monastery at Campagna. He was forty-nine.

The Dominicans had been open to adopting Aristotle's logical method, and thus Aquinas's own ideas. But during Aquinas's Paris days, the Franciscans had resisted the subservience of Christian dogma to the pagan philosopher. Not long after Aquinas's death in 1274, rumors began to emanate from Paris that Christian orthodoxy had been contaminated by Aristotle and his Arab interpreters, and the systematic thought of Aquinas—soon to be called Thomism—came under this same suspicion. The rumors finally wafted south, as they usually did, to Rome.

The pope asked the bishop of Paris to begin investigating the new trends at the University of Paris—a development that would lead to perhaps the greatest intellectual upheaval of the Middle Ages. In 1277, the bishop of Paris issued his report, a condemnation of 219 theses promulgated by the "schools." The bulk of those condemned were Averroistic, but many overlapped the writings of Aquinas. A few days after the action in Paris, Canterbury's Archbishop Robert Kilwardby—a Dominican who had once taught in Paris—issued similar condemnations. Both Franciscan and Dominican clerics were convinced that philosophy had tainted theology. They wanted to thwart Aristotle so naturally took aim at Aquinas. Closing off these philosophic avenues of inquiry (with their Greek and Arab origins) was a turning point in medieval theological debate, and opened the way for the growing influence of the Franciscans in England, who had arrived there only a half-century earlier.

A FEW years before Aquinas was born, a group of four Franciscan friars crossed the English Channel and established the new order on England's soil. The expedition of 1224 was led by the Italian friar Agnellus of Pisa, who landed at Dover with three priests and five laymen. They moved on to Canterbury to lodge at the Dominican hospice. From there, two English members of the group proceeded to London and then to Oxford, due west of the city.

Oxford, first spoken of in English chronicles in 912, had been settled on a shallow cattle crossing of the Thames. A fortress was built but the town remained rural for generations. It never had a cathedral as a base for a school, so its future as an educational hub was hardly foreseen. But by 1117, chroniclers spoke of a "master at Oxenford" who was known as a teacher, and lecturers trained in Paris began to arrive in great numbers. By the end of the twelfth century the Oxford schools swelled to three thousand students. When the first two Franciscan friars arrived on a rainy night in 1224, the town had been established as an academic center for over a hundred years.

The two friars were well received. They were given a parish house and by summer had set up operations in a donated cluster of land and buildings inside the city walls. They opened an infirmary, and in 1244 King Henry III gave them permission to pull down a section of the city wall to expand. The Franciscans eventually created a small suburb of Oxford, its crenellated wall stretching down to the River Thames and the property eventually taking in an island as well. Erecting a church, monastery, and chapter house, the Franciscans prospered. Flush with the things of this world, they were forced to wrestle with their vows of poverty. They also grappled with the lust for knowledge, for many of them, after hearing impressive visiting "lectors," wanted to attend cathedral schools or even university at Oxford or Paris.

The Franciscans were earnest missionaries. One of their most important converts was Robert Grosseteste, the first chancellor of Oxford. Early in the settlement process, the Franciscan leader Agnellus had "besought Master Robert Grosseteste of holy memory to lecture to the friars," according to a chronicler. "Under him they made exceeding progress in a short time both as to their sermons and as to those refinements of manners which are suitable for preaching." Grosseteste inaugurated his lectures in 1225. In 1235, he became the local bishop, seated in Lincoln. He bequeathed his library to the Oxford Franciscans.

Over the next few generations, the standard of Franciscan education improved at a rapid pace. The Franciscans began to handpick their best talent to earn bachelor's or master's degrees at Oxford. As at Paris, the secular faculty began to bicker with the religious orders flocking to the city. When the Franciscans tried to establish Friar Thomas of York in a chair of Holy Scripture in 1253, the Oxford establishment protested that he did not have a liberal arts degree. An exception was made, but a new statute declared that no one could teach theology "unless he had graduated in Arts in some University and read one book of the Canon or of the *Sentences* and publicly preached in the University."

The Franciscans resisted these demands far more strenuously than the Dominicans, but eventually they came around. In 1320, the Franciscans submitted to the Oxford standards. From then on, candidates were selected by the religious order or by the pope, who issued *statuta papalia* that enabled them to study. In 1336, Pope Benedict XII decreed that no friar could receive a bachelor's degree unless "he had first lectured on the four books of the *Sentences* with writings of the approved doctors." With its great library and its proximity to the university, the Franciscan house in Oxford became the center of an educational system that spread in England and north to Scotland.

IN 1277, as the great heresy charges were being issued in Paris and Oxford, a young Scotsman named John Duns entered a Franciscan monastery. By now, a stream of notable Franciscans had begun to protest the dominance of Aristotle and Aquinas—that is, the dominance of philosophy itself—in the realm of Christian doctrine and belief. After 1277, philosophy and theology began to move even further apart; just as Aquinas had tried to unite them, Duns Scotus—"Duns the Scot"—worked to separate them once again. Theology "will get nowhere with heathen philosophers," he insisted.

Born and educated in a Scottish town called Duns on the English border, Duns Scotus began his studies at Oxford in 1288. He did three years of postgraduate work in Paris and then returned to Oxford, where he graduated in 1301. During his lifetime—he died in 1308—he would master the empiricism of Grosseteste along with the Platonism of Augustine and his Franciscan followers; write the required commentaries on Aristotle; and give a notable series of lectures on Lombard's *Four Books of Sentences*. His attempt to hammer out a middle way between the extremes of the Franciscans and Dominicans earned him the nickname the "Subtle Doctor."

As a student in Paris, Scotus had found himself in the midst of a heated political dispute between King Philip IV (the "Fair") and Pope Boniface VIII. Since the days of Gregory VII, more than a century earlier, the powers of the papacy had waxed and waned, and Boniface was determined to reassert those powers. He challenged the French king's ability to tax bishops. In

1301, the year Scotus finished at Oxford, Boniface excoriated Philip for putting a bishop on trial in a royal court. The next year he took a step unprecedented in the papacy. He summoned the French bishops to a council and afterward issued the bull *Unam Sanctam*, which claimed that the papacy has ultimate authority in no less a realm than the universe itself. Earthly powers are judged by spiritual ones, it argued, and "it is altogether necessary to salvation for every human creature to be subject to the Roman Pontiff."

While he was working on a graduate degree in Paris, Scotus had taken up residence in the Franciscan monastery by the university, which stood on the south bank of the Seine. He began to lecture on the *Sentences* and took part in some disputations. By spring term of 1303, Scotus had participated in a few famous formal disputes and was wrapping up the term's lectures on the *Sentences*. At that moment, King Philip was setting up his own council to depose the pope. In June 1303 the gardens of the Louvre Castle, across the river from the university, filled with a great anti-papal rally. It opened with a procession of friars and was addressed by a bishop who was a former chancellor of the university and by four leading Dominicans and Franciscans.

The next day, the king's agents visited the Franciscan monastery to interrogate each friar on his support for the king. The French friars vowed allegiance, but more than eighty others—typically foreigners such as Scotus—dissented. For this, they were summarily

expelled from Paris and given three days to leave. Scotus
was exiled to England. Several months later, allies of
Philip attacked Boniface's palace outside Rome and
held him for three days until local forces freed the pope.
He returned to the city and, shaken by the incident, died
three weeks later. The next pope made amends with
Philip, and in the spring of 1304, Scotus was allowed
to return. In 1305, doctorate in hand, he was appointed
Franciscan regent master in theology at Paris.

For his innovations, Scotus became for Franciscans
what Aquinas was to the Dominicans—their most
famous philosopher. He was no less an Aristotelian
than Aquinas, but he was trying to solve a new set
of problems. Like Aquinas, Scotus fell in the camp
of "moderate realism"—the idea that there were real
essences outside the mind, but not in the extreme sense
taken by Platonists and Augustinians such as Anselm.
Furthermore, some Franciscans had emphasized cer-
titude in knowledge only by divine illumination, or
as Augustine had put it, that "no pure truth can be
expected from sensation." Scotus more or less agreed
with Aquinas, who had argued along with Aristotle
that "nothing is in the intellect that has not first come
through the senses."

Scotus knew this convention well enough, but he
was in a mood for revolutionary thinking, especially
after the famous heresy charges of 1277 had rocked
the universities and monasteries of Europe. One condemnation concerned the thesis, implied by Thomas

Aquinas, that individuals were merely clumps of matter. If true, was there any essence to individual things? The debate was on. Some philosophers agreed with Aquinas that a thing was defined by the fact that it was made of matter; others said the quantity, or amount, of matter was the key definition of a thing. Still others defended essences, or defined each thing by its direct relationship to God. Scotus walked into this minefield offering a compromise. A human being and a tree, for example, both had matter and quantity, but what made them different as individual things—say, Thomas Aquinas and an oak tree—was an "essence" of humanness and treeness, but also what Scotus called a particular essence, or "thisness." The universal part of a thing was the "common nature" it shared with others, but its "thisness" was known by the immediate "intuitive cognition" of the human mind. Scotus's distinctions were incorrigibly subtle, but upon "thisness," future thinkers (like William of Ockham) would build an empirical view of individual objects, a stimulus to modern science.

Scotus had embarked on a program of simplification. He accepted Anselm's idea of God as a perfect being but argued that the concept of God as *infinite* being was still "simpler than the concept of good being, true being." Anselm had argued that God's actions were governed by cosmic reason, an idea Scotus rejected: in his view, God could do absolutely anything except engage in self-contradiction. The God of Scotus was absolutely free and willful, not a god who did what

Anselm called the rational and "fitting" thing. For Aquinas, God was known indirectly as a first mover: Scotus asserted that it was "a more perfect and immediate" knowledge to know God as ultimate Being.

Scotus stressed the power of God's will to determine not only the existence of each thing, but also what was right and wrong in any given situation. For the scholastics, "the good" was defined by moral legislation; for Scotus, it was defined by the Legislator. Over a few generations, the scholastics had expanded their legislative idea by building upon Aristotle's tradition that reason led to the virtues necessary for a good life. Aquinas added other moral and supernatural virtues. The result, however, was that well-meaning scholastics multiplied one virtue after another into an impossible web of moral logic and rule-making.

To cut through this complexity, the Subtle Doctor produced what would come to be called "Scotus's rule": seek the most economic description. Scotus reduced the number of virtues to seven. Critics accused Scotists of being zealous simpletons, envisioning a world in which God acts by an arbitrary will, individuals are the only realities, and dogmatic faith the only religious response. Scotus had tried to separate theology from philosophy, but many of his followers took only the theology part, leaving reason behind. During the Renaissance, the humanists began to deride the dogmatic followers of Scotus as "Duns men," or "dunces," as the term evolved.

But the sophistication of the Subtle Doctor was never in doubt for anyone who actually read his work. He was one of the last great scholastic defenders of "universals" as a reality that stood behind individual things—that "humanness" and "treeness," in the mind of God and in metaphysical reality, made the individual named Thomas Aquinas and the oak tree on an English hillside possible as things in the world. Scotus did his work one generation after the departure of Aquinas, the greatest theologian of the late Middle Ages. In the tradition of disputation, he used his predecessor as a foil for his own arguments. Now it was time for Scotus to become the foil. As he lay dying in Cologne in 1308, another young scholar was rising in the ranks at Oxford, a Franciscan named William of Ockham. Ockham took what he liked from Scotus, and then—as every new generation will—launched his own revolt. Aquinas had rejected Anselm's proof of God; Scotus (who accepted it) took exception to Aquinas. But all three agreed on one thing: the universe was indeed connected by essences, logic, and the mind. William of Ockham begged to differ.

CHAPTER 5

Ockham's Razor

THE village of Ockham, a day's ride southwest of London, entered the chronicles of history around 1288, with the birth of a boy named William. The village, with a population of just four hundred, had been named either for its oak trees or for an ancient chieftain. Whichever it was, when William reached fourteen, his parents brought him to London to start life as a monk. Of seven Franciscan centers in England, London was the second largest, after Oxford. William joined the Gray Friars, named for their gray frocks.

The monastery was a busy crossroads of new recruits, young lectors making the rounds, and the best and brightest Franciscans crossing between Oxford and Paris for university studies. William's family may have spoken French or Middle English. But as his education commenced, he began to converse and write in Latin, the universal language of the learned. When William—who would become known simply as "Ockham"—was about eighteen in 1306, he was ordained as a subdeacon by the archbishop of Canterbury. The date is one of the few that are certain in the life of one of the most influential Franciscans of his century.

LONDON
OXFORD
PARIS
MUNICH
AVIGNON
ROME

AGE OF OCKHAM
1288 - 1348

It was the dawn of the fourteenth century and, as in prior centuries, in Ockham's time the papacy vied for power with kings, two kings in particular: the king of France, who was audacious enough to capture and hold the pope for a few days, and the German king. Still holding onto the aura of Holy Roman Emperors, the German kings invaded Italy on and off throughout Ockham's lifetime, attempting to put the papacy in its place. Pope Boniface VIII (of *Unam Sanctam* fame) was presiding over a kind of apogee of the papacy, the last flourishes of its medieval glory. Although this mood of papal absolutism was soon to wane, its influence on Scotus and Ockham was indelible. They both envisioned an absolute God and a world of contingent things.

Though Ockham was an atrocious writer of Latin prose, he lived in Europe's first epoch of poetry. Romantic stories hinted at by Islamic verse found during the Crusades were elaborated on by French troubadours. And while Ockham studied in England, Dante Alighieri wrote in Italy. Composed between 1308 and 1320, Dante's *Divine Comedy* was the most popular book of late medieval Europe, the crowning glory of medieval scholasticism. In its pages, Peter Lombard and Thomas Aquinas were duly at rest in Paradise, giving the whole tradition of textbooks, sentences, and summas an ethereal majesty.

Dante and Ockham were only about twenty years apart in age, and were united in their political fortunes. Both took up politics when philosophy failed, and both found themselves in exile late in life. But they were worlds apart in their philosophies. Dante's work popularized Thomism as the apex of medieval philosophy. Ockham's legacy was to revive a kind of nominalism that struck at the very roots of the scholasticism that had given Aquinas his fame. The two men initiated their exploits in the early fourteenth century, a kind of proto-renaissance, a time during which scholasticism was already beginning to break up, despite Dante's labors to romanticize the great ideas of Thomism for future generations.

Amid this ferment, young Ockham found himself a student at Oxford, pursuing a bachelor's degree. Each year, the English Franciscans sent a couple of the top students to the University of Paris, but though Ockham never received this honor, Oxford ranked second only to Paris, and swarmed with several thousand students. They collected around Balliol and Merton colleges and witnessed the building of University Hall. The king and the bishop of Lincoln watched over the school but, given the students' high spirits, were unable to prevent the occasional riot.

As a student, Ockham first had to prove that he was intellectually capable of an academic career. This was done in the well-worn tradition of lecturing on the Bible and Lombard's *Sentences*, and so he began. Besides Lombard and Aquinas, the name that dominated his small Franciscan world was Duns Scotus. Ockham was not a student of Scotus, but he heard the

Subtle Doctor's lectures as he passed through London. Most important, Ockham chose Scotus to be his philosophical rival. To make his new ideas absolutely clear, Ockham set up Scotus as his "principal adversary," according to one historian. The first battlefield was Ockham's lectures on the *Sentences*.

Ockham delivered these maiden lectures between 1317 and 1319 at Oxford and the London monastery. These were three very productive years for the young Franciscan scholar, and he kept careful records of his lectures for publication. Around 1321, the Franciscans appointed Ockham as a formal teacher.

As he awaited approval to receive his doctorate, Ockham wrote a major treatise on logic, the *Summa Logicae*, or "summary of logic." The entire system of Thomas Aquinas had been built on the logic of Aristotle. Even Scotus had perpetuated this system. But Ockham followed Scotus on only a few points: an impulse to simplify the world (though his was a simplicity that would have horrified the Subtle Doctor), and an emphasis on the absolute will of God. What Ockham rejected was the argument, which originated with Aristotle, that the mind, the world, and God were all connected. He thus freed himself to study the simple logic of the relationships among solitary things.

Ockham had begun to lay out this detour from the Aristotle-Aquinas tradition in his very first commentary on the *Sentences*. Now he carried the attacks into public disputation, and soon enough, this brought trouble to his door. Among the scholars of the time, the Dominicans were the most loyal to the system of Aquinas. But some Franciscans began to worry about Ockham's ideas too, since he dared dispute even the great Scotus. In 1322, the Franciscan regent master at Oxford, John of Reading, traveled on business to the papal court in Avignon. There, he warned its theologians of a possible troublemaker: Ockham.

Ockham's theology was actually quite orthodox when it came to dogmas of the faith, acknowledging as it did miracles and supernatural accounts of God's actions in the Bible. But he had tampered with old methods and traditions, especially Augustinian and Aristotelian orthodoxies. In the eyes of his contemporaries, he had undermined scholastic reasons for dogmas, especially the scholastics' belief in universals.

For a start, Ockham knew exactly what Scotus had been trying to do in his theology, philosophy, and logic. Scotus felt it was obvious that universals exist in the mind of God and thus organize the nature of the world. So the big question for Scotus was, 'How do individual things exist?' Given that groups of things share a "common nature," Scotus concluded that individuals must exist through a kind of separate "thisness." From Ockham's point of view, Scotus asked the wrong question. Individual things were easy to explain. Universals were the problem. To Ockham, universals looked not only suspect but entirely useless as well.

In his charmingly blunt manner, Ockham said that universals are "absolutely false and absurd." He was a habitually plainspoken man. "This I say," he declared, "that no universal is existent in any way whatsoever outside the mind of the knower." For Ockham, universals were merely helpful names—or *nomina*—inside the mind. They were rhetorical tools but not real "substances" outside the mind. Besides, he said, the use of universals to explain the world implies many contradictions. It was a debate that had begun with Plato's assertion, transmitted by Augustine, that the "ideals" of all things—man, tree, beetle, chair—preexist, so the things in the world are merely shadowy representations. Such Platonic ideals or essences, according to Ockham, are in effect singular things, but are also claimed to be many separate, particular things in the world—a clear contradiction. In other words, these universal ideal essences lost their universality in the world. Defenders of universals, he concluded, were perpetually mired in trying to explain the one and the many, the thing in itself, and the idea that different types of things share a common nature.

The Ockhamist solution was to define the world as a collection of radically individual things. Each thing's existence—each beetle, each chair—depended solely on the will of an almighty God.

In an age inclined to simplification, it was hard to think of a simpler universe than the one described by

Ockham. In ethics, Scotus had proposed his "rule" that the fewest possible number of human virtues should be identified as real. But now, Ockham applied the vaunted "razor" of later legend to all of reality. Ockham's Razor cuts away unnecessary explanations in search of the simplest possible one. Scholasticism had already argued that every claim about the world must be backed by an adequate explanation and evidence: biblical revelation, experience, insight, or logical deduction. Ockham refined this claim, cutting metaphysical reasoning from the list of acceptable defenses. As he said in two different places, but always in awkward prose:

> Nothing must be affirmed with a reason being assigned for it, except it be something known by itself, known by experience, or it be something proved by the authority of holy scripture.

> We must not affirm that something is necessarily required for the explanation of an effect, if we are not led to this by a reason proceeding either from a truth known by itself or from an experience that is certain.

Ockham was clearly not a skeptic, a view typified by such extreme slogans from the ancient Greeks as, "Nothing is known." He believed in knowledge and in the things of this world while asserting that, for any given problem, the simplest, most concrete solution was always the best. As he put it, "What can be explained by

the assumption of fewer things is vainly explained by
the assumption of more things."

Ockham's program of hyper-simplicity spilled over
into his explanation of language as well. Nominalism
was, after all, given its name because it said universals
are nothing but words—indeed, hot air, a mere emis-
sion of sounds, a *flatus voces* to some. Ockham elaborated a theory of words and language to a far greater
extent than had his nominalist predecessors. He asked
himself, "What does a word stand for?" Human beings
and animals both make sounds in response to particular realities. But only the human mind, it seems, makes
sounds about abstractions. Hence, human language is a
collection of words acting as "signs" for things, abstractions, or the relationships between them. For all the
power that words possess, they are not tied to eternal
essences—they are only tools of the mind.

For Ockham, the word "God" stood for a singular
Being. But where Augustine and Anselm had suggested
that the word evokes an actual contact with God's
nature, either in the soul or mind, Ockham stopped
short. He found this notion impossible, for he believed
that God is approachable only by faith. In his quest to
simplify, Ockham held out a God that is beyond not
only reason, but beyond all possible conception. God
can be known only in contrast to the shifting, unreli-
able world of objects, and this helps to define God's
absolute existence and freedom to do what he wants.
To follow through with this logic, Ockham proposed a

remarkable theory of how the mind knows things. He said the mind can perceive illusions as real things if God wills it. For example, he asked "whether intuitive cognition can be had of an object that does not exist." The answer was yes: "Even if a thing has been destroyed the intuitive knowledge of it may be given to us," he said. "Intuitive cognition of a nonexistent object is possible by the divine power." Whatever God can produce by a physical law he can also produce by sheer will.

Ockham's universe of "things" was so entirely empirical that it helped to stimulate the rise of medieval science, but the God he presented was so willful and arbitrary that the cosmos seemed anything but scientific. Beyond mere nominalism, he produced an "Ockhamist" outlook that was a unique combination of philosophy, science, and theology. An Ockhamist believed in a world of radical things, a God of *potentia absoluta*—the power to do anything short of a contradiction—and the religious response of faith, for the mind could not know God. It was a view adopted by many leaders of the scientific revolution during the Enlightenment, including Isaac Newton.

Ockham's rejection of the old metaphysics of universals—a belief that neatly connected the mind, words, and God's reality—made him skeptical of proofs of God. He found none decisive, although some impressed him as more plausible than others. The idea of God as conserver of the universe had merit, and so did a hierarchy of goodness. But Ockham also acknowledged that the universe could be eternal, and that even if a "cause," or creator, were proven, that cause might be many gods and not just one. He eventually quoted Anselm's definition of God, probably from Aquinas's *Summa*, and seemed at first to agree. "We could go on *ad infinitum*, if there were not some one among beings to which nothing is prior or superior in perfection," he said. Then he rejected Anselm like all the rest: "But from this it does not follow that it can be demonstrated that there is only one such being. This we hold only by faith."

Moving from one kind of proof to another, Ockham showed his dissatisfaction. He left no doubt about the sad limitations of the human mind when it came to the divine. "I say that neither the divine essence, nor the divine nature, nor anything intrinsic to God, nor any thing that is really God, can be known by us without something other than God being involved as object," he said. (One of his examples was God using a burning bush to address Moses). He also insisted that the immortal soul, which the Aristotelians and Thomists believed was the "form" behind matter, could not be proved. "There is no way," he writes, "of knowing with clear certainty either by reason or experience that such and such a form is within us, or such and such a soul is in us, or that such and such a soul is the form of the body." As always, "We hold these three truths by faith only."

The soul, the triune God of Christianity, and all else proclaimed as church doctrine rested on belief, not logical proof. Ockham perpetuated Scotus's program of separating philosophy from theology. Philosophy began to resemble empirical science. Theology turned to faith, dogma, and the Bible. Ockham had little to offer budding metaphysicians—those who, like Anselm, wanted to find all the connecting parts of a rational cosmos. Instead, Ockham foreshadowed a "faith alone" future. For this, some historians have called him the "first Protestant."

Around Oxford University in 1320 were gathered Thomists, Augustinians, and now nominalists. But no one had yet conceived of a Protestant, even if such seeds were being sown in people like Ockham. The absence of the word, however, did not obviate the consequences. By this time, Ockham's teachings were stirring up controversy within the Franciscans, in addition to the resistance he met with from Thomists and Aristotelians. Though his course of study has led historians to believe that he fulfilled the requirements for his doctor's degree, or Magister Theologiae, it seems that Ockham was blocked from obtaining a position on the theology faculty. Whatever his rank, he would soon earn the moniker "Venerable Inceptor"—taken to mean candidate or initiator—and he become infamous beyond England, achieving a reputation that finally reached the papal court in the south of France and, in the longer run, spawned an "Ockhamist" movement.

When Ockham was finally summoned to the papal court to account for his ideas, he found himself thrown into the fractious world of European politics. It was also a time when the colorful images of Dante's *Inferno*, *Purgatorio*, and *Paradiso* began to shape the European imagination. In the bitterness of political exile from his hometown of Florence, late in life, Dante had placed a few popes in hell—the same popes with whom Ockham would take issue. But Dante had magnanimous moments, too, and it was perhaps during one of these that he placed the great medieval intellects in his fictional Paradise. When Dante journeyed to Paradise, he found the Franciscan Bonaventure telling a sympathetic story about Dominic, who founded the Dominicans, and the Dominican Aquinas telling an equally sympathetic story about Francis, who founded the Franciscans.

Thus *The Divine Comedy* portrayed a future time of peace between the two religious orders, despite their sometimes-contentious debates over Thomism, Scotus, and the new philosophy of Ockham. As Ockham traveled to Avignon, however, the bigger political issue seemed to be the growing split among the Franciscans themselves. They were at odds over their doctrine of "evangelical poverty." The doctrinal dispute had become deeply political, and as Ockham headed south, the tensions across Europe were high, fueled by zealous friars, opportunistic princes, and an Avignon papacy eager to show its authority.

CHAPTER 6

The Nominalist Terror

THE papacy began to build its case against Ockham around 1322. The catalyst had been John of Reading's visit to Avignon, and his complaints of dangerous innovation. At the same time, the chancellor of Oxford, John Lutterell, a zealous Thomist, was ending his short but stormy tenure in that position, apparently ousted by the bishop after a campus row could not be resolved.

Lutterell, still ambitious to serve the church, asked the king of England for permission to transfer to Avignon, scene of the papal bureaucracy. The king was not eager to have rumors of Oxford disputes spread widely, and at first refused. When he finally relented, Lutterell got permission to work abroad for two years, a period the pope was quick to extend.

The first assignment Lutterell received, upon his arrival in Avignon, was to comb through Ockham's published commentary on the *Sentences*. Word had circulated that Ockham challenged the very Aristotelian categories on which Thomism, and thus Catholic theology, rested. The papal court never shied from theological and political combat, but under the reign of Pope John XXII, an autocratic, octogenarian canon lawyer who had ascended to the papacy, it was especially aggressive. Lutterell was eager to make a contribution. He applied his Thomistic ardor to investigation of Ockham's writings. In August 1323 he produced fifty-six opening charges of heresy. Before the year ended, Ockham had received his summons.

He left England in May 1324, crossing the channel and landing at Calais, from where he began the trip southward to Paris, and then farther south, following the Rhone Valley for more than three hundred miles to Avignon. There, the river was bisected by Avignon's famous twenty-two-arch bridge, the only crossing south of Lyons. For two centuries, pilgrims from Italy had headed for Avignon to ford the Rhone on their way to Spain, an important spiritual destination since Anselm's time.

Approaching Avignon, Ockham's first sighting would have been the bridge and the great spur of rock around which the city was built. Compared to London or Paris, he might have felt this was still a provincial outpost. But the papacy had been there for fifteen years and would be for another fifty-five, and whatever its size, Avignon was fast becoming a hub of European affairs. Italian banking houses had followed the papacy to southern France, and Avignon had become a city of money changers and trade, its markets and homes filled with fine fabrics, tapestries, breads and wines, and fish from the coast. The money built libraries and opened a university. The papal palace, which before the court's arrival had been occupied by the local bishop, grew continually in size and opulence. By the time Ockham had arrived, Avignon was beginning to merit the Italian poet Francesco Petrarch's later description of it as a city of venality and corruption.

Ockham was entering a new world. Lodged at the Franciscan residence, he was forbidden to leave the city, but at least he wasn't imprisoned. There was much to fill his time: the French papacy had built ties with the University of Paris, and Avignon bustled with teachers and theologians from that city. As Ockham soon realized, however, many of these same scholars, with their general Thomistic bias, were also investigators and advisors to the courts, some of them members of his heresy commission.

The commission looked into only three of Ockham's four books of commentary on the *Sentences*, but nonetheless the work dragged on interminably. To start with, Lutterell had written up a *libellus*, or "bill of charges." Its accusations ranged across most of Ockham's novelties in philosophy, logic, and doctrine. Lutterell declared that Ockham was worthy of censure in all these areas, but the commission was only concerned about theology.

In an age of Thomism, Ockham was not questioned so much on belief as on definitions, the curse of scholasticism. How did Ockham define *merit* and *reward*, *grace* and *justification*? What was his logic on whether Christ had the human ability to sin? How did he define *necessary* and *contingent* when it came to what was possible or impossible for God? The commissioners measured Ockham's answers against Aquinas's *Summa Theologica*, a rational system favored by the commissioners. (One of them, a Dominican, saw things Ockham's way, but mainly because he so admired Scotus's work on God's freedom and will.)

Worst of all, Ockham was charged with a cover-up. In that age of durable animal-skin parchment, scribes with razors routinely scraped off the ink to replace old writing with the new. The authorities looked closely at the Ockham parchments and came to the conclusion that he had razored away his heretical words, especially in the section concerning the key theological issue of his case: the Eucharist. This was not the first time the Eucharist had gotten a scholastic thinker in trouble—it had been a point of contention between Lanfranc and Berengar—nor would it be the last. Ockham's sin was his nominalism: in paring down the Aristotelian categories, he had excised the notion of quantity, which played an important role in the prevailing theological explanation of how Christ existed in the bread.

The commission took so long, however, that both its members and the subject of the investigation himself were distracted by other events. All of Avignon, and indeed much of Europe, watched as two great political tides swept simultaneously into the corridors of the papal palace. The first was the papacy's ongoing rivalry with Italian nobles and the German king, from both of whom it was still in hiding. The second was within the church itself: Rival wings of the Franciscan order were tearing the landscape apart with their disagreement over the meaning of *poverty*, the founding principle of their increasingly powerful religious movement.

John XXII had ascended to the papacy just as the German throne was in dispute. When Louis IV of Bavaria finally got the upper hand in 1323, John rejected his claim to be Holy Roman Emperor. Louis, in turn, declared John an antipope. John then excommunicated Louis. Both sides were looking for allies. Louis seized upon Dante's work, *De monarchia*, circulating its anti-papal argument widely. He also turned an interested eye on the now-volatile Franciscans.

All Franciscans of the day, including Ockham himself, were well versed in the issues and conflicts over the doctrine of poverty. Though the historical record is far from clear, Ockham may have spoken publicly on the topic during his journey across France. If rumors of such a speech reached Avignon before him, Ockham would have arrived with the halo of an agitator.

The doctrinal upheaval had roots stretching back to within fifty years of the Franciscan order's founding, when a wing of zealous purists known as "spiritu-als" advocated not only poverty but a kind of spiritual anarchy. The leader of this evangelical cause was the charismatic Joachim of Fiore, who made apocalyptic predictions of an impending spiritual age. The move-ment was an intellectual crucible for the doctrine that Christ and his apostles did not *own* anything. Under the decrees of two previous popes, Nicholas III and Celestine V, the spirituals—now popularly called "zealots"—believed that the papacy *owned* Franciscan resources, thus keeping the order itself pure. But such a purist doctrine was bound to cause strife. The struggle between zealous factions was especially acute in Italy.

On ascending to the papal throne, John XXII decided it was time to put an end to the dispute. As far as he was concerned, this was an entangled administrative and theological matter. The idea that the pope owned Franciscan property to free the order of sin struck John XXII as impractical and absurd. He reversed his predecessor's policy. And in 1323—as he was dispensing with Emperor Louis as well—he issued the papal bull *Cum inter nonnullos*, declaring that the doctrine of Christ's total poverty was heresy.

A practical man, John XXII wanted to make the Franciscans manage their own affairs just like every other commonsense religious order. They should be stewards of God's property, just as Christ had been a steward of his own earthly belongings. He did, however, have another agenda: the proud pope aimed to strike at the Franciscans' pride. The doctrine of evangelical poverty was the most prominent example of the Franciscan conceit that it was the purest order of all, purer even than the papacy itself.

The Franciscans were powerful contenders on both the political and spiritual battlefields. As John XXII issued his bull, the international order elected as its Minister General a friar named Michael of Cesena, a noted champion of evangelical poverty. Michael called an order-wide "general chapter" meeting in Perugia, at which the friars resolved to dispute the papal rulings. Michael fixed his signature on that decision. Dissenting from the pope was risky enough, but to do so publicly begged for a confrontation. Michael was summoned to Avignon to explain himself. When he rode into town in December 1327, Ockham had been there, waiting on his heresy commission, for more than three years.

It is likely that Ockham had sided with Michael of Cesena during the years of the brewing controversy, but he had kept his deepest loyalties a secret. Now Michael came to him for help, requesting that Ockham research the background of the poverty debate. What had previous popes said? What had John XXII done and how? Ockham's previous absorption in universals and things, necessity and contingency, evaporated in the face of the most explosive theological question of his age: what happens when the pope himself falls into heresy?

Shortly after his arrival, Michael of Cesena met the pope in an audience and defied him openly. Michael was detained, and the pope retired with his advisors to make a plan. In April 1328, the papacy condemned the Perugia declaration and ordered another general chapter assembly to depose Michael and elect a new Franciscan leader. While Ockham had not yet been formally charged in his heresy case, there could be no doubt now that he belonged to the anti-papal camp. He was no less in danger of losing his life and liberty than was Michael of Cesena. Michael had composed a protest of the papal ruling that deposed him and planned to disappear when it was made public. When he did, Ockham and two other friars went with him. On the night of May 26, 1328, the foursome snuck out of their residence, reportedly stole horses, headed for the wharf, and navigated a boat down the Rhone River.

All the while, the shrewd Emperor Louis the Bavarian watched the Franciscan debate as it tore apart Italy. Louis, whether out of sincere belief or political expediency, sided with the spirituals. He also found an ally in the Italian political thinker Marsilius of Padua, one-time rector of the University of Paris. Marsilius had come to his attention when, in 1324, Marsilius published the stunning treatise *Defensor pacis*, which advocated a secular curb on the papacy. As Michael of Cesena and William of Ockham made their escape, Emperor Louis invaded Italy. He entered Rome on April 13, 1328, with Marsilius, now his spiritual advisor, at his side. They found a schismatic Italian friar, a spiritual Franciscan, and installed him as Nicholas V. The event was a religious fiasco, but Louis got what he wanted: a pope who acknowledged him as emperor.

Michael of Cesena and his companions headed for Italy—in all likelihood, this had been the plan all along. Two weeks later they met up with the emperor's entourage at Pisa and continued with Louis on his trail north. By now, Ockham had come down firmly on the side of separating the church from temporal governance in the world. As tradition has it, at the meeting in Pisa, an exhausted but resolute Ockham declared to Louis: "O Emperor, defend me with your sword, and I will defend you with my pen."

The Avignon papacy acted swiftly, excommunicating the fugitives on June 6, while they were still at sail. The document suggests that Ockham was found guilty of heresy in both his writings and his sermons. The next year, in 1329, the Franciscan general chapter met in Paris. It deposed Michael of Cesena, who was on the campaign road with Emperor Louis and still possessed the official Franciscan seal. The chapter also began to systematically expel all the pro-poverty "Michaelists." By the time they succeeded, Michael and Ockham had been settled in Munich, Bavaria, for about a year. Ockham set to work with a vengeance on a collection of political tracts.

He spent a furious three months writing the *Work of Ninety Days*, his first essay against the pope and in defense of the poverty doctrine. These early writings were personal. His *List of Papal Errors* pulled no punches, listing seven heresies of which the pope was guilty. The writings that followed rallied Christians against illegitimate papal authority. Only after Pope John XXII died in 1334 did Ockham take a step back. Though he then began to dissect papal power more generally, he never offered exact specifications for a doctrine of church and state or described in detail a political system. In fact, he never quite rejected papal authority.

Modern historians have seen Ockham in a variety of lights. He has been associated with Marsilius's total rejection of papal power in *Defensor pacis*, but also with Dante's support for good popes who hewed to spiritual matters. Some have viewed Ockham as primarily a theologian. He grappled with monastic poverty, spiritual freedom, and the heresy of higher authorities. Others have seen him as striking the death knell of papal power—another reason he is called the "first Protestant." A final view takes Ockham to be a "constitutional liberal" who advocated a friendly division of duties between state and church.

Whichever legacy holds true, in his day Ockham was under the strain of local events. His political writings exude self-interest. He needed a king's "sword" to protect him, so he happily defended the imperial throne. He backed German political leaders who rejected a papal role in secular elections, and he defended the adulterous marriage of Louis's son as a necessary political expedient, not the moral business of the church.

Despite living his final twenty years in Munich, Ockham never learned German. He communicated only in Latin, and, in his isolation, did enjoy some contact with the Franciscan chapter in southern Germany. Ockham probably traveled to other meetings in nearby Switzerland. And, of course, he had the companionship of Michael of Cesena, who died in

Munich in 1342 with the seal of the Franciscan order still in his possession. He bequeathed it to Ockham for safekeeping. Emperor Louis died in 1347 and with him Ockham's sense of security.

His first move was to return the Franciscan seal to the bona fide Minister General. A Vatican document was prepared, but whether Ockham ever signed it is unknown. Only the text remains: it testifies to Ockham's belief "that the Emperor has no authority to depose the pope, Pius Pontiff, and to elect and create another," and contains a promise that the signatory will be "faithful to the Pope" in the future. The document is interesting for its exclusive focus on political "heresies"—Ockham's philosophical and theological teachings go unmentioned. It is the last record we have of him. Ockham died during the Black Death epidemic of 1347–50, and was buried at the Franciscan monastery. Centuries later, his body was relocated, and its whereabouts are still unknown.

As the Franciscan upheaval demonstrated, ecclesiastical and secular authorities in fourteenth-century Europe were near equivalents of each other. Even monastic scholars could be drawn into the fighting in the streets. In his twenty years in exile, Ockham took on three successive popes: a public theological duel of unprecedented length—at least until the Reformation. In this, Ockham joined the literary world of Dante, despite the contrast between the poet's eloquent Italian and Ockham's inelegant Latin. Their works are among the most colorful records of the late medieval papacy, on the eve of even stormier days of schism and rebellion. Dante consigned three popes to hell, including John XXII. Ockham charged them with heresy and tarnishing an otherwise holy office. In other ways the two men were at odds. Dante, trained by members of the Dominican order, lionized Aristotle, Aquinas, and thus the tradition of universals, metaphysics, and proofs of God. Ockham reserved his praise for nominalism in philosophy and science, and faith alone in theology.

Whatever the relative strength of their philosophies, Dante outflanked Ockham in the popular world by the sheer power of his poem. *The Divine Comedy* became so influential in medieval culture that Aristotle and Aquinas seemed to have won the day: God had placed Thomism in Paradise and nominalism in Purgatory.

But Dante's was not the whole story. Ockham's nominalism smoldered in monasteries and universities across Europe. In 1339, the whispers of his influence at the University of Paris grew loud enough to attract the pope's notice, and the papacy condemned the nominalist teachings the following year. The more extreme nominalists whom Ockham inspired suffered a similar fate. Nicholas of Autrecourt had pushed nominalism furthest. He was a true skeptic: only "things" could be known, he maintained; nothing of origins, causes, or effects. Eventually, Nicholas too was summoned to Avignon. He was given thirty days' notice, but when the ruling looked as if it would go against him, he fled to the German emperor's domain. The next year, lacking Ockham's resolve, Nicholas returned to Paris. He recanted and burned his writings in public.

Despite the papacy's best efforts, the influx of Ockham's English texts could not be easily stopped. As they came under deeper study in Paris, the secular arts faculty took particular interest. Although an Ockhamist school emerged, Ockham was only one source—empirical science, humanist letters, and the first glimpses of skepticism were also percolating in Europe—in the expanding *via moderna* as it began to rival the *via antiqua*, the scholasticism of Aristotle and Aquinas. The nominalists picked and chose the emphasis they liked.

For those intrigued by the new vision of an absolute and arbitrary God, as limned by Scotus and Ockham, there could be no better confirmation than the Black Death. It swept across Europe, ruthless and arbitrary, heedless of even the most pitiful appeals for miraculous intervention, bringing to an end the literary and contentious age of Dante and Ockham. The scholastic's rational and hierarchical universe, organized around essences, virtues, and logic, made no sense in the face of the ravenous disease, which reduced Europe's population by nearly half.

For others, the appeal of Ockham's legacy was the nominalist use of language and its ability to put an end to universals. In the late fifteenth century, when the nominalist masters at the University of Paris were again defending themselves against charges of impiety, they explained that they sought only a superior way to that of the "realists," who followed the *via antiqua*. Nominalists, the scholars wrote in a defense addressed to the king of France, "show diligence and zeal in understanding all the properties of terms on which the truth and falsity of a sentence depends. But the realists neglect all these things."

Equally important, however, was nominalism's role in preparing the way for empirical science, in particular new theories of motion. The idea of "impetus"—inspired by the Aristotelian notion of objects' having purposes and being moved by these purposes—was eventually replaced by the more accurate notion of "inertia," that a body will move straight forward until influenced by another body. This was first applied to motion on earth, then to motions of the heavens. The study of the heavens, of course, prompted perhaps the greatest revolution in the history of science, culminating in the great discovery that Earth and the other planets moved about the sun and are simple objects governed by empirical laws.

Although Ockham had learned something about empiricism from the Franciscans at Oxford, the study of the natural world was not of particular interest to him. Still, he did influence science, if only in the way that scholars of the later Middle Ages appropriated his work. For Ockham, the theories or models of science were fundamentally just another form of abstract language trying to take individual things—that is, things governed by an absolute God—and generalize their relationships into groups or laws. However, Ockham would not concede that the human mind could decipher the laws of nature as if they were essences. The most the mind could do was to invent generalizations, or models, that helped to organize the objects in the physical world. In short, nominalism was the opposite of the purist mathematical science that emerged in the seventeenth century. This science would attribute to geometry and other systems an eternal existence, with their origin, presumably, in the mind of God—a notion that would have been anathema to an Ockhamist.

DESPITE Dante's heroic poetry, the vision of a great metaphysical system began to unravel in a universe newly dominated by nominalism. That universe offered little of the security of the past. Nominalism presented a universe of pieces, not of wholes. No single system could any longer be used to explain theology, nor was there much explanation for the newly fluid European landscape, crowded with cities, transient individuals, leveling commerce, petty politics, and ever-new gadgets and inventions.

For those who needed certainty, Ockham's God of absolute will was the only thing on offer. In the earlier medieval world, God had been absolute, but he had ruled by way of systems, gradations, and even logical formulae. Now, God was pure and absolute volition, ruling all things individually and inscrutably. In so contingent a world, the more piously inclined looked to their Bibles and to faith alone, which would become a cardinal slogan of the Reformation.

Another response to the changes afoot was a revival of humanism. The achievements of Leonardo da Vinci, Machiavelli, and the de Medici family typified a new belief in art and invention. It was the age of the individual, who would battle not with God's providence, but with fortune; man was the measure of all things. The ideal of human action derived from classical myths. These Renaissance heroes did not seek metaphysical explanations to life, but rather pursued a lust for life itself, hoping their names and honor would survive in statues, books, and chronicles.

On the sidelines of this glory-seeking stood the skeptics, a humanist movement that also had roots in the Greek past. With its tenet that only objects can be known, nominalism verged on skepticism. But Ockhamists at least had God's revelation to lean on, while what might be called "secular" skepticism had cut itself loose from theology and dogma. Even among Christian intellectuals, however, skepticism found its place. Desiderius Erasmus, the Dutch Catholic and literary virtuoso, used skepticism in his famous work, *In Praise of Folly* (1509), to satirize a corrupt church. A generation later, the French lawyer and essayist Michel Montaigne, who like Ockham was inclined toward "faith alone," used skepticism to free himself of the great burdens of doctrine, metaphysics, and the sectarian wars of his century.

Montaigne relished a calm and tolerant curiosity about the world, asking, "What do I know?"—a motto that impressed a future countryman who also became enamored of skepticism, René Descartes.

STOCKHOLM

AMSTERDAM

LAFLECHE   PARIS   FRANKFURT   PRAGUE

TOURS   NEUBERG

AGE OF DESCARTES
1596 - 1650

CHAPTER 7

Descartes's Dream

In the summer of 1619, a young soldier named René Descartes wandered through Frankfurt, a city on a plain by the River Main, distinguished by its twin-cupola City Hall and red-stone cathedral named for Saint Bartholomew. He was there to witness the coronation of the Holy Roman Emperor, a title still used with calculated exaggeration by Ferdinand II, the king of Germany. The streets were filled with royal pomp and popular drunkenness. The Thirty Years War had just broken out, and the battles skirted the edge of Germany. The devastation it would bring could hardly be imagined on so cheerful an August day.

Among the crowds, Descartes must have looked like any other young soldier, except for his long black hair and rakish mustache. He had been working as a gentleman soldier for a year and a half, and possessed the financial means to wear something a bit dashing and to own a fine sword. He'd begun his career as a border sentry in Holland, where the Calvinist Dutch, in alliance with the French Catholics, were blocking the expansion of Spain's Catholic empire. Eventually he made his way east and joined a Catholic military force in Bavaria.

When Descartes left Frankfurt, heading back to the army barracks some two hundred miles away, winter weather descended heavily on the open countryside. By the time he reached Neuberg, a little county on the Danube, he was forced to make camp. He rented a small cabin. He was cold and alone. As he told future readers: "Finding no conversation to divert me, and otherwise, fortunately, having no cares or passions that troubled me, I stayed all day shut up alone in a stove-heated room where I had complete leisure to converse with myself about my thoughts."

Descartes had been educated by the Jesuits, a new movement born during the Catholic Reformation. They had seized hold of Thomist philosophy and were perpetuating the scholastic tradition throughout their expanding educational system. As a young boy, Descartes had studied all the great questions—from Anselm to Aquinas to Ockham—and, in his solitude by the stove, he began to look for his own solutions. On the night of November 10, 1619, he had three dreams, which he took to confirm his destiny as a new kind of philosopher and scientist. He was "full of enthusiasm, carried away completely by the thought of having discovered the foundations of a marvelous science."

He reports that the dreams were so palpable that he awoke more than once in surprise. In one dream he felt pain in his side. In the next he was assaulted by sparks and a whirlwind, and passed through baffling episodes in which books disappeared and people he knew passed by as if ghosts. Finally, he dreamt of a poem by the Latin poet Ausonius, "What road in life shall I follow?" But the young man remained uncertain of how to spark his new revolution—the embryonic idea of using mathematics, skepticism, reason, and faith to find absolute certainty—and resumed his journey home when the weather cleared.

While on sentry duty in Breda a year earlier, he had met, quite by accident, a Dutch intellectual named Isaac Beeckman, a doctor, Calvinist minister, educator, and dabbler in optics and the new mathematical, mechanistic sciences. In the noisy street of the border city, he and Beeckman had stopped at the same public notice board to read a mathematical puzzle that had been nailed up, a problem of intersecting lines in space. Now came a letter, a year later, in 1619, with this encouragement from Beeckman: "May God grant that we may live together for some considerable time to penetrate to the core of the Kingdom of science."

Descartes had just turned twenty-three, and the attention of the scholar, some seven years his senior, made a strong impression on him. Altogether, the events of 1619 sent him on a path of discovery not unlike that of Anselm, who left Aosta at about the same age. Ockham had been in his mid-thirties when his new teachings prompted heresy charges, and Descartes was about that age when his writings risked the same fate. He too would innovate, and pay the usual price. Not the least of his troubles came as a result of his revival of the Ontological Proof of God, and how he used it to unravel the medieval synthesis—of which Anselm and Ockham had been a part.

DESCARTES was born in 1596 in the Loire Valley, not too far south of the monastery at Bec. He was reared in a Catholic family in a little village by the River Loire, surrounded by vineyards and wheat fields. His mother died in childbirth when he was still young, and, distant from his father—a tax collector for the crown—Descartes turned to his maternal grandmother and nursemaids for affection and stability.

The practice of law was a family tradition, and little René's destiny seemed at first to be no different. Like his older brother, he was enrolled in a prestigious new school, La Fléche College, founded by the Jesuits. The order had a strong international outlook, and this made its members suspect in nationalist Catholic countries. In France they had criticized King Henry IV, who had converted to Catholicism to take the throne, and were subsequently expelled just before Descartes's birth. But they had returned and opened La Fléche in 1604, housing it in a chalet with classically geometrical gardens—and winning King Henry's patronage.

Descartes spent nine years at the school and was exposed even at a young age to the political, religious, and scientific upheavals of his day. In 1610, Henry was assassinated by a fanatic who opposed the king's tolerance of Protestants. The school came to possess the king's embalmed heart, and for years afterward, students watched as it was carried in ceremonial procession from the parish church to the college chapel. Henry's death marked the end of religious accommodation to Calvinists, a sectarian conflict used shrewdly by the rising political figure Cardinal Richelieu, who became premier in 1624.

The religious climate of the time was still set by the Council of Trent, which had inaugurated the Catholic Reformation in the face of the Protestant movement. Trent not only spurred a revival of scholasticism, but decreed that the physical sciences fell under the "faith and morals" of the church. The new science of the time was astronomy. Copernicus's *On the Revolution of the Heavenly Spheres*, first published in 1543, was beginning to have real influence. In Descartes's lifetime, the budding science reached a final conflict with church authorities in the person of Galileo Galilei. But in the first years of the seventeenth century, La Fléche celebrated the sciences, including Galileo's discovery in 1610 that Jupiter had orbiting moons. Science was still seen through the lens of scholasticism—as the Jesuit syllabus said, "in matters of any importance let [the professor] not part from Aristotle."

Descartes's studies at La Fléche exposed him to the rudiments of hydraulics, clocks, pumps, looms, and other devices of scientific interest. Just north of La Fléche lay the great "robotic" gardens of the Saint-Germain estate. While still a young man, Descartes would have ambled over its grounds, with their Italian-style gravel paths, fountains, basins, and grottos, and seen the hydraulically driven statues of humans and animals. Reportedly, they moved, danced, played music, and made sounds as if speaking. This mechanistic landscape made an impression.

In time, Descartes mastered both Latin and his native French, and developed personal habits that would shape his life. For reasons of health, he was instructed to stay in bed until late in the morning, and preferred to do so for the rest of his life. He learned the mental art of meditation devised by the founder of the Jesuits, Ignatius Loyola, who had developed "spiritual exercises" that used visualizations of the life of Christ as a focus of thought and devotion. His education also included study of the Latin-French dictionary, the poet Virgil, the Roman rhetorician Cicero's *Letters*, and the *Adages* of Erasmus; at some point Descartes must have read Montaigne. But even as students pored over the *Guide for Sinners*, studied the severe life of Ignatius, and followed the Jesuit syllabus, they also experimented with recitation and theater. Descartes carried the metaphors of the stage into his life's work. "Actors, taught not to let embarrassment show on their faces, put on a mask. I will do the same," he wrote in an early notebook. "So far, I have been a spectator in this theater which is the world, but I am now about to mount the stage, and I come forward masked."

After graduating in 1615, Descartes enrolled in law at the University of Poitiers and graduated in a year with a degree in civil and canon law, but did not go into practice. "As soon as I had completed the course of study at the end of which one is normally admitted to the ranks of the learned, I completely changed my opinion," he recalled. He had the luxury to do so, for as lower nobility, he had a source of family income, could use the title "Monsieur," and lived and traveled with a valet. He moved first to Paris, but as the conflict between Spain and the French-allied Dutch continued, he headed north to fulfill what he felt to be his duty—working as a gentleman soldier, riding with an army—at least for a time.

After concluding his service in Bavaria, Descartes resolved to see what he could of the world, in hopes of throwing some light onto his philosophical project. At first, he headed toward Paris, but warnings of the plague made him detour, and he returned home, taking advantage of the opportunity to settle some of his family's financial affairs. In the spring of 1623, he traveled through the Alps to reach Turin to look into a more lucrative military appointment, such as in the officers' corps. It is generally thought that he made his first and only visit to Rome the next year, and, taking the Cenis Pass, returned to France. By 1625, Descartes had moved to Paris, where he spent the next four years, his longest stay in the great city of culture and contention.

In his later writings, Descartes told the story of these formative years. He had "roam[ed] about in the world, trying to be a spectator rather than an actor in all the comedies that are played out there." He avoided battlefronts, cities with plagues, and conflicts with the church. His quarry was the "great book of the world," and his code of life was to stay unobtrusive, living by the codes of his host countries, and by stealth when necessary, according to his motto: "He lives well who is well hidden." His intellectual code was to take nothing for granted, to get rid of all past opinions. He vowed "never to accept anything as true if I did not have evident knowledge of its truth." He resolved to include "nothing more in my judgements than what presented itself to my mind so clearly and so distinctly that I had no occasion to doubt it."

Before long, Descartes had abandoned any idea of being a professional soldier or seeking a government office: he wanted to be a philosopher—a synonym for scientist in those days. He resolved to "devote my whole life to cultivating my reason and advancing as far as I could in the knowledge of the truth, following the method I had prescribed for myself." Method—that was the key. He was hardly alone. New books abounded. There was Jerome Sanchez's *Admirable and General Method for Learning all the Sciences more Easily and Quickly*, Della Porta's *Twenty Books of Natural Magic*; Johannes Kepler's *New Astronomy* (1609) and *Harmony of the World*, the latter published in Prague when

Descartes was in Frankfurt. Above all, there was the English statesman Francis Bacon, who wrote the *New Organon* of 1620. Bacon rejected Aristotle's deductive method, which began with first principles. Bacon offered instead an inductive method, which began with the evidence of individual things. On this point, Descartes found himself divided. He too was passionate about rejecting Aristotle, but he also was a deductive thinker: deduction was the method that yielded mathematics and the Ontological Proof of God. Descartes wanted to start fresh. As he wrote later, "My whole aim was to reach certainty—to cast aside the loose earth and sand so as to come upon rock or clay." Now, having just turned thirty, Descartes tested his personal philosophy in the culture and salons of Paris.

The Paris of his day was stylish and cosmopolitan, though in the summer a foul smell blew off the Seine, and when it rained, the streets were thick with mud. Still, it was a vibrant city. The Catholic Reformation couldn't quell the spirit of lively debate. The Jesuits, who were Thomists, took on the Jansenists, who were Augustinian in theology. A nationalist French church clashed with international Catholic movements that pledged loyalty mainly to the papacy. Meanwhile, in the secular realm, skeptics and "libertines" were beginning to form a new generation of writers, thinkers, artists and experimenters, who looked to the growing nobility for wealthy patrons.

Descartes shrank from such social climbing, perhaps because of his early failures to find congenial appointments as a government lawyer and tax collector, like his father, or as a military officer. He lived instead on his inheritance. In Paris, he reportedly fought a duel over a lady but finally said "truth" was more beautiful than any woman. He put most of his energy into navigating among the most powerful intellectual groups on the scene, which, besides the Thomists and Jansenists, included the nominalist skeptics, the advocates of mechanical science, and mystical societies like the Rosicrucians.

The skeptics had become known as Pyrrhonists, after the Greek skeptic Pyrrho of Elis, proudly repeating his slogan that "nothing is known, and that it is permitted to doubt everything." The mechanists argued that the universe was composed of an infinite number of "atoms," nothing but corpuscles in empty space. This was the view Descartes's friend Beeckman espoused, and it was gaining adherents in Parisian circles. Doctors took seriously the theory of the English physician William Harvey that the heart pumped blood like water in pipes. The vaunted age of the machine was trumpeted around Paris in the 1624 book *The Explanation of Moving Forces, with various machines, both useful and decorative.* Mechanism made good sense to Descartes.

Concerning the mystics, Descartes's spoken convictions were firm. He was dismissive toward a popular mystical work, Ramon Lull's *The General and Ultimate Art,* or *Brief Art* as it came to be known. "I do not want to construct a Lullian Brief Art," Descartes wrote Beeckman in 1619. Instead, he wanted to construct "a completely new science by which all questions that can be raised about any kind of quantity, either continuous or discrete, may be solved by a general method." The new science was geometry: a reduction of all physics to size and quantity. Nonetheless, mysticism was in the air, and its influence can be subtly read in some of Descartes's future ideas, such as the separation, or "dualism," of mind and body.

From his days at La Fléche and the University of Poitiers, Descartes had personal connections enough in Paris, but it was the new acquaintances that remained significant. He came to know some of the leading Jesuits and would have liked to have friends at the Sorbonne, now the leading school of the University of Paris. Its theologians were the gatekeepers of philosophical orthodoxy in France. The closest connection he made was with a priest named Marin Mersenne. A professor of theology, Mersenne had moved to Paris in 1619 as a member of the Minims, a reformist order of Franciscans.

Orthodox in his belief, and a defender of the Aristotelians at the Sorbonne, Mersenne knew the usefulness of both skepticism and science to informed argument. His attitude toward metaphysics was mildly skeptical, and he seemed open to a range of specula-tive works in science. His lifelong project was to rebut the Protestant charge that Catholics were befuddled by "magic"—the doctrine of the existence of miracles. Mersenne argued that Catholicism took the mechanistic laws of nature seriously. Miracles were only the rare suspension of those laws.

For thirty years Mersenne stayed in touch with the serious intellectual developments of his day. He acted as a kind of human telegraph system in Europe. As the Dutch statesman Constantijn Huygens would say, he "filled the air of the universe with his letters." As their friendship deepened, Mersenne would become Descartes's chief informant about Europe's intellectual trends, and a vigorous advocate of his still-unpublished work.

In the autumn of 1627, Descartes was invited to attend a lecture at the papal diplomat's estate. The speaker was Chandoux, a noted chemist and alchemist (later executed for counterfeiting). With great flourish, Chandoux attacked the Aristotelian system. He offered instead a version of a skeptical mechanistic universe. In this universe, Chandoux said, probability was the highest order of knowledge, not certainty. Chandoux's position was hardly radical at the time, and after the lecture, everyone was full of praise—except Descartes. He was asked to explain himself.

As the story is told, Descartes made the argument that it was possible to go beyond mere probability and have "clear and distinct" ideas, the sort of knowledge typified by mathematics. Though he had been put on the spot, Descartes was pleased with his own philosophical performance: in later correspondence he described his presentation as "better established, more true, and more natural" than Chandoux's. Among those who heard it were Paris's leading intellectuals. Mersenne was there, as was the founder of the Oratory, one of the powerful Catholic reform movements.

The tenacious Cardinal Pierre de Bérulle had founded the French Oratory in 1611 on the model of the original one in Italy, which was dedicated to religious argumentation against unbelievers and Protestants. A kindly-faced, mustachioed Augustinian who favored mystical prayers and the doctrines of the anti-Thomist Jansenists, Bérulle was impressed by Descartes's new method and approached him with questions. (The conversation also likely included an attempt to recruit Descartes for the Oratorian cause.)

The distractions and frivolity of Paris were beginning to grate on Descartes's nerves. He wanted to escape the city and the tentacles of the various Catholic movements, so zealous in their recruitment. He later wrote of "distancing myself from my acquaintances, in order to lead a more tranquil and peaceful life." His project to write a list of thirty-six rules explaining his universal "method" had ground to a halt; it was only a group of papers and notes when published, posthumously, as *Rules for Guiding One's Intelligence in Searching for Truth* (1684). An essay on geometry on which he had been working did not bear fruit until 1637. He was interested in refracted light and had learned to grind lenses to study it, but he was as yet no expert.

In France, moreover, religious strife was inescapable. Cardinal Richelieu's political machinations had increased tension between Catholics and Protestants, and in late 1628 Descartes witnessed one of its tragic consequences while on a short trip to La Rochelle with the mathematician and military engineer Gerard Desargues. The dominantly Calvinist city of the Huguenots, or French Protestants, had long been an object of Catholic resentment, and since the previous year, a Catholic army had laid siege to La Rochelle. Descartes had visited at the attack's tail end, probably to see the dike the military had built around the city. During its last holdout, fifteen thousand Huguenots starved to death. When the survivors finally surrendered, the army entered and Richelieu celebrated a High Mass in the cathedral.

BACK in Paris, Descartes had followed the protracted debates over proving God and the soul, so he decided to find his own solutions. He realized that to defend his mechanistic conception of the universe without skeptical or impious argument, he needed to formulate a new metaphysics. Upon leaving France, he made his next home in the far north of Holland, in the city of Franeker, which he chose for its university and experts in mathematics and lens grinding. He lodged in the small castle of a local family and soon wrote a friend that his first project would be a "little treatise" on metaphysics.

His letters to Mersenne and Beeckman reveal his excitement over his progress. To Mersenne, he wrote that he had "[set] out to prove the existence of God and of our souls when they are separate from the body, from which their immortality follows." To Beeckman, he wrote that it was a project to "demonstrate metaphysical truths" for his new science. "The first nine months that I spent in this country, I worked on nothing else." But in October 1629 the project was eclipsed by a new enthusiasm.

Since his early lessons in lens making, Descartes had been fascinated with optics. The study of light revealed to him a universe guided by logical geometric principles. When corpuscles of light hit lenses, water, or rainbows, under close observation they could reveal the nature of matter. While in Franeker, Descartes received a report of stunning interest to mechanists trying to understand the physics of light. In Rome, the astronomer Christoph Scheiner had observed "parhelia," or false multiple suns, a rare optical event caused by ice crystals in the atmosphere. Intrigued, Descartes abruptly dropped his metaphysics. He returned to his work with lenses and optics, and eventually anatomy, going daily to the butcher for animal parts to dissect.

The next four years, between 1629 and 1633, were perhaps Descartes's most innovative in the sciences. They were also very transient years. He moved four times—from Franeker to Amsterdam and then on to Leiden, Denmark, and Deventer. He asked Mersenne not to reveal his whereabouts. In these years, Descartes formulated his own physical and metaphysical description of the universe, and he put it down in a work titled *The World*. The project grew and grew. "Instead of explaining a single phenomenon, I have decided to explain all natural phenomena, that is, the whole of physics," he wrote Mersenne. "And the plan gives me more satisfaction than anything previously, for I think I have found a way of presenting my thoughts so that they satisfy everyone, and others will not be able to deny them."

The flow of letters to Mersenne continued. In early 1630 the work was "going very slowly." He was "now studying chemistry and anatomy simultaneously." And it was far easier to study than to write, he admitted. In December he again had "countless different things to consider all at once." He hoped to "give a true account without doing violence to anyone's imagination or shocking received opinion."

The entire project, completed mostly between 1630 and 1633, had two parts: *The World, or A Treatise on Light*, a basic physics of the universe, and the *Treatise on Man*, a mechanistic view of the body, perception, and biological vitality. Descartes did not want to "shock" anyone. So he softened the mechanistic blows by inviting readers to consider his new world as an imaginary kind of space, what he once described as "the fable of my *World*." *The World* summed up the physics that was the foundation for all Descartes's later work. He presented both cosmological and biological phenomena as machinery, if more hydraulic and protean than clock-like.

Descartes rejected "atomism," the ancient Greek notion that the universe was composed of an infinite number of indivisible atoms filling empty space. Instead, he boldly declared, matter occupied all of "space"—matter itself *was* space. Matter expressed itself in corpuscles of three kinds, from fine to rough, with no empty space between. Matter operated by pure geometry: each corpuscle moved in a straight line. It moved in this way because God, who was immutable, ordained that motion from the dawn of the universe. As Descartes wrote later, "God imparted various motions to the parts of matter when he first created them, and he now preserves all this matter in the same way."

Descartes's vision in large part was typical of Enlightenment mechanism; the will of the Creator was viewed as integral to sustaining the world machine. What Descartes did differently was to use the principle of inertia to explain all circular and complex movements. Each corpuscle moved in a straight line until deflected by other matter. The universe therefore moved like a dense liquid, finding inertial pathways in circular forms. Based on the fineness or coarseness of matter, bodies orbited each other. This created a cosmos of "vortexes." One of these was the Earth and other planets circling the sun.

Although Cartesian physics is fanciful in some respects, to his credit, Descartes did propose a law of inertia, the heart of the later Newtonian revolution. He offered a mechanical explanation for planetary orbits and a physical definition of light: fine particles that peeled off the spinning sun. The *Treatise on Man* applied mechanics to the physical body and sense perception. As if fresh from a visit to hydraulic robots in the gardens of Saint-Germain, Descartes described the body's vital functions as a flow of matter in pipes.

The chief flowing medium was blood, which also carried a finer substance that Descartes called "animal spirits." This subtle matter connected the brain, and therefore thoughts and moods, to nerves and to muscles. He inferred that the pineal gland— the seat of the brain—was where the immaterial soul made contact with the body; this gland filtered animal spirits into the blood. Perception, he claimed, was the pressure of light corpuscles on the eye and nerves, and this in turn was carried to the brain, and back, by animal spirits. When sensory perceptions arrived in the brain in great number, they formed a "common sense." Animals (which he called "machines") also collect sense data; but only humans integrate it by the power of a rational soul, which is embedded in an immaterial substance created by God—a "thinking substance."

Throughout *The World*, Descartes had trod on delicate theological territory. He had risked a new description of the created universe. He had rejected Aristotle's use of "final causes" to explain the particular motions and directions of objects and replaced Aristotle's notion of the "souls" of objects with simple matter that, colliding with itself, produced shape, direction, individual beings, and life itself. He rejected Aristotle, but he also rejected nominalism, arguing that eternal truths could be known with great certainty, while "things"—made not of atoms, but indefinite divisions of matter—were ambiguous until given certainty by reason, mathematics, and metaphysical principles.

Descartes's God, like the God of nominalism and skepticism, was free, and in his freedom governed and sustained the universe. But where the nominalist's God was capricious, Descartes's ruled by means of constant laws that were rational, or "clear and distinct" when considered by an unprejudiced mind. For Descartes, the human will too was free. But free will could lead to error in judgment—the reason precise knowledge was so hard to obtain, he argued. Error could be overcome by the disciplined, proper use of the mind, the cultivation of a rational soul that opened up the metaphysical order of the universe to the philosopher.

Early in 1633, Descartes wrote Mersenne that he was finishing up *The World*. He hoped to send him a copy as a New Year's present as 1634 approached. But then bad news arrived from Italy.

AS Descartes began *The World*, Galileo finished up his *Dialogue Concerning the Two Chief World Systems*, a project on which he had labored from 1624 to 1630. In this work, Galileo presented evidence that the Earth moved around the sun: the tides, the annual orbital motion of the Earth, its diurnal rotation, and the changing path of sunspots. It was a radical challenge to Aristotle's eternal universe anchored on a stationary Earth.

Published in Florence in March 1632, the *Dialogue* was quickly censured. On July 23, 1633, the cardinals in charge of the Roman Inquisition condemned the work. The Inquisition in Florence had warned him as early as 1616, but the ebullient and stubborn Galileo continued to write. The 1633 ruling did not presume to judge Galileo's work by the "natural light of reason"— it used the church fathers' decree at Trent that natural philosophy, or science, "cannot err on dogmas of the faith."

Descartes, who had heard the news both from local booksellers and in a letter from Mersenne, knew immediately that his own work, which also showed the Earth moving about the sun, was in trouble as well. "I nearly decided to burn all my papers, or at least let no one see them," he wrote Mersenne in November 1633. He could not believe that the well-connected Galileo, a friend of the pope, could be condemned for simply asserting that "the earth moves." But the church had spoken, and Descartes sounded shaken: "I must admit that if this view is false, then so too are the entire foundations of my philosophy." He did not relish a showdown with the Inquisition. "So I prefer to suppress it rather than publish it in a mutilated form."

Mersenne proposed a clever solution: why not publish it in discrete pieces? Over the next three years, as he moved between Amsterdam, Utrecht, and Leiden,

Descartes extracted smaller essays from *The World*. There was one on refracted light, titled *Dioptrics*: one on geometry; and a third on the weather, titled *Meteors*. His *Dioptrics* advanced the study of refracted light; *Geometry* proposed a general algebra for quantity and space, while *Meteors* explained the bow in the rainbow. In all, they presented a full vision of Descartes's mechanistic universe—except for its application to the Earth and the human body.

Mersenne helped Descartes plan for their publication. At his urging, Descartes wrote a preface on metaphysics, which served to ground his science in the theology of the day and explain his method. He gave the preface a title of its own: *Discourse on the Method for Conducting One's Reason Well and for Seeking Truth in the Sciences*, now considered one of the short masterpieces of Western philosophy.

In 1033, Anselm was born in the Alpine valley of Aosta, Italy, where the high peaks and Roman ruins, such as this ancient amphitheater, stirred his young imagination with ideas of God above and political power below.

The 1066 Norman invasion of England, illustrated in the panels of the Bayeux Tapestry, opened the way for Continental monks such as Anselm—then a thirty-three-year-old monastery prior in France—to enter English affairs of church and state.

The Cluny monastery in France was the hub of the eleventh-century reforms to strengthen the papacy. Anselm bypassed Cluny but became entangled in the affairs of Pope Urban II, seen here consecrating the great Cluny church in 1095. From a twelfth-century manuscript.

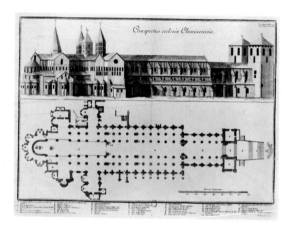

*The grounds of the Cluny monastery were so vast in its heyday,
and so filled with monks, pilgrims, and travelers, that visitors
across those centuries called it "heaven on earth." From a
seventeenth-century engraving.*

Anselm became archbishop of Canterbury in 1093, a story told by his biographer, Eadmer, and recreated in this etching (1864). King Rufus, on his presumed death bed, forcefully "invested" Anselm as archbishop, a secular intrusion central to the twelfth-century "investiture controversy."

As abbot of Bec monastery, Anselm wrote meditations, prayers, and his "proof" of God in the Monologion and Proslogion. Years later, he delivered a collection of his works to Countess Matilda of Tuscany, as portrayed in this twelfth-century illuminated manuscript.

Anselm's adventure became well known after his death through the Life of Anselm, *written by his assistant, biographer, and scribe, Eadmer. In this illuminated manuscript of that work (c. 1200), Eadmer is seen writing inside the "Q" while Anselm stands on a hapless monk, serving as the "I" that starts a new paragraph.*

No authentic image of William of Ockham survives, but this color drawing from a Franciscan monastery at Kraków, Poland, from the fifteenth or sixteenth century, illustrates the marks of a learned monk in cowl and cape.

Iodoci Ba. Ascensii.ut boni iuuenes ad litterarū studia feruētius incūbāt cohortatio:cū ǭdā huius opis & clarissimi uiri Iohānis de trittenhem abbatis i spanhē cōmēdatiūcula.

Ingenui iuuenes faris melioribus orti:
Quis acre ingeniū iuppiter ipse dedit:
Pellite segnitiē ueteresꝗ reuoluite libros
Quoꝗ:instar licitū ē cōdere cuiꝗ nouos.
Edite quo noscāt uixisse aliquādo miorest
Triste etēm totū ē morte migrare uirū.
Nec mihi ti ignaua quisꝗ formidine dicat:
Quid faciā? uacā acta petisse sciam.
Scilicet egregii periere uolumina Crispi
Et bona pars Plauti i diaꝗ uerba Titi.
Deniꝗ sueterū repetas monumēta uirorꝝ
Heu quota quaꝗ extet portio codicibus
At nihil excuses transacti obliuia secli:
Nec belli rabiem nec rapidi astra poli
Perpetuū siquidem cūctis extantibus euū
Mira impressores arte dedere libris.

Ecce mō arguti liber optatissimus ockam
In quo de uariis queritur hæresibus:
Et maiestates papalis & imperialis
Pensantur trutinæ lancibus æquiferæ
Atꝗ incredibili panditur dexteritate:
Vnde aliis uisum ē hiscere grāde nephas
Is liber inquā olī iā multū optamus amici
In spanhemēsi ouat patris abire finū.
Nēpe uiri auspicio tā magni ēditus:orbē
Terrarū/exigua sperat obire die .
Nā neꝗ germanis studiosis charior alter
Nec magis heroum dignus amicitia.
Illū & magnifici ꝓceres mirātur & omnis
Vr patriæ partem religiosus amat.
Proide moret mīme qū nfo multa labori
Illius accedant cōmoda præsidio.

William of Ockham wrote his lengthy Dialogues *as if a student probed a scholar on the topics of heresy, the papacy, and politics. After the printing press, the book was mass produced and its frontispiece (c. 1494) showed a seated student interrogating the scholar at his lectern.*

ABOVE: *Ockham dissented from Thomas Aquinas (center) on proofs of God and from Pope John XXII (bottom left) on "evangelical poverty." This 1365 Italian fresco, "The Triumph of Catholic Doctrine," arrays the friends and foes of Aquinas, whom John XXII made a saint in 1323, just before Ockham was charged with heresy for his "nominalism," which soon shaped Europe.*

OPPOSITE: *Aquinas's commentaries on Aristotle's works were widely published in the Renaissance and Reformation. The title page of this 1575 book pictures Aristotle with cap and beard and offers Aquinas's Christian analysis, titled* Commentary on the Four Books of Aristotle's "On the Heavens and the Earth."

S. THOMAE
AQVINATIS
IN QVATVOR LIBROS ARISTOTELIS
de Cœlo, & Mundo Commentaria,

Quæ, cum morte præuentus perficere non potuerit,
absoluit Petrus de Aluernia:

CVM DVPLICI TEXTVS TRANLATIONE,
Antiqua videlicet, & IOANNIS ARGYROPILI noua,
diligenter recognitis,
QVÆ OMNIA NVPER SVNT MAXIMA DILIGENTIA CASTIGATA.

*Duo item Indices nunc addits sunt, alter librorum, ac lectionum summas continens,
alter Commentariorum scitu digna demonstrans.*

VERA ARISTOTELIS STAGIRITAE EFFIGIES PERIPATETICAE DISCIPLINAE PRINCIPIS

VENETIIS,
APVD HÆREDEM HIERONYMI SCOTI,
M D LXXV.

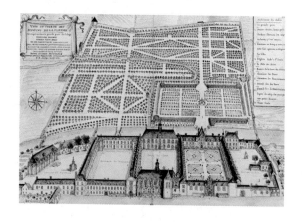

The Jesuits, exiled from France, returned to found La Fléche College (seen in a 1655 engraving). René Descartes attended for nine years until 1615, learning Aristotle and theology, but later hoping to dethrone Aristotelianism with a proof of God and a mechanistic universe.

Puis le diametre de ce verre n'a pas befoin d'eftre fi
grand que pour la lunete precedente, ny ne doit pas
Voyés en
la page
126. auffy eftre fi petit que celuy du verre A de l'autre d'auparauant. mais il doit a peu prés eftre tel que la ligne
droite N P paffe par le point bruflant interieur de l'hy-
perbole N R P: car eftant moindre, il receuroit moins
de rayons de l'obiet Z; & eftant plus grand, il n'en receuroit que fort peu d'auantage; en forte que fon efpaiffeur
deuant eftre a proportion beaucoup plus augmentée
qu'auparauant, elle leur ofteroit bien autant de leur force que fa grandeur leur en donneroit, & outre cela l'obiet ne pourroit pas eftre tant efclairé. Il fera bon auffy
de

Descartes censured his 1633 book, The World, *which said the
Earth moved, but later published its contents under cover of a
metaphysical essay,* Discourse on Method *(1637). One chapter,
"Diapotrics," was on optics, illustrated by light diffracting in a
compound telescope.*

ABOVE: *The Dutch painter Frans Hals painted Descartes in 1648 or 1649 but the original is lost. This copy in the Louvre is considered an accurate likeness of the philosopher, aging under his fine black wig.*

OPPOSITE: *Descartes proposed a unique view of a mechanistic universe, in which all of space is filled with grades of matter, moving in circles—or vortexes—and causing Earth to circle the sun, as illustrated in his 1644* Principles of Philosophy.

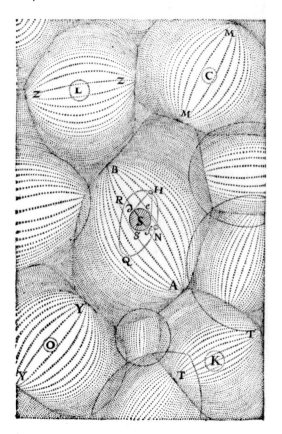

Unheralded in France and Holland, in 1649 Descartes sought royal patronage from the Lutheran court of Queen Christina of Sweden; as this eighteenth-century painting depicts, he served as a teacher of geometry. He died a year after arriving, buried in a pauper's graveyard.

CHAPTER 8

"A Thinking Substance"

As it turned out, the seven years after the Galileo
debacle were the happiest of Descartes's life. While
boarding at a professor's home in Amsterdam in 1635,
he took up with the housemaid, Helene, with whom
he had a daughter named Francine. For reasons of
social taboo and snobbery, Descartes and Helene never
married. They traveled as gentleman and maid with his
supposed niece—revealing the truth only to a Calvinist
minister who baptized Francine in the Reformed
Church—and probably raising some local gossip as
they set up house on the Dutch coast, near Haarlem,
where they remained until 1639.

The completion of the *Discourse*, his first public
work, added to Descartes's satisfaction. It had been his
aim to write a popular work in French, and at the time
"popular" meant memoir, a form recently advanced
by Michel Montaigne (he of "What do I know?" fame)
but dating back to Augustine's *Confessions*. Descartes
made his *Discourse* autobiographical, and his charming approach boosted, in the long run, France's reputation as a nation of letters. The *Discourse on Method* also
marked the first appearance of the maxim for which
Descartes would become famous. In his quest for cer-

tainty, Descartes said, he had to start by doubting absolutely everything. What he was left with, the only thing in the world he found himself incapable of doubting, was his own doubtful thought. And since there was thought, there must be a thinker—hence, 'I think, therefore I am.' As he explains: "And observing that this truth *'I am thinking, therefore I exist'* was so firm and sure that all the most extravagant suppositions of the sceptics were incapable of shaking it, I decided that I could accept it without scruple as the first principle of the philosophy I was seeking."

Once that assertion was made, Descartes moved on to his first proofs of God, all of which hinged on the "idea of a being" that was God. He was entering the philosophical territory in which an "idea" proved a reality—a very Anselmian, a priori, first principles, axiomatic, and deductive kind of approach. But the proof he first offered in the *Discourse* is not what one might expect of a so-called heir to Anselm. Descartes offered a traditional, *a posteriori* proof more typical of Aquinas: all things have causes, so the perfect "idea" of God must have a perfect source outside the human mind, which is imperfect. His own finite and imperfect mind could not be the cause of such an idea. Descartes writes, "So there remained only the possibility that the idea had been put into me by a nature truly more perfect than I was and even possessing in itself all the perfections of which I could have any idea, that is—to explain myself in one word—by God."

In other words, perfections that he knew about, but which he did not himself produce, must have an external source. "There had of necessity to be some other, more perfect being on which I depended," Descartes said. Clearly he was moving in the ontological direction.

The main message of *Discourse* was that skepticism could be defeated. In that triumph, moreover, certainty would be restored, beginning with the utterly distinct and clear idea that "I exist." It is therefore somewhat ironic that Descartes was inclined to present his theories as speculations. He often spoke of his theories as fables, and *Discourse* similarly offered "imaginary spaces" or a fable-like "new world" to readers. Descartes presented his models as hypotheses, not as unmitigated proof. In this, his technique was markedly different from that of Galileo, whose style of argument was direct and pugnacious. Descartes's techniques kept his works from official condemnation by the church— at least while he was alive.

Despite this care, however, Descartes's attempt to conceal the fact that he himself had written a heretical work was almost comical. He spoke of Galileo as "someone else." After looking at that someone's theory, "I had noticed nothing in it that I could imagine to be prejudicial either to religion or the state." In a masterpiece of evasion, Descartes maintained that he wanted to explain the laws of nature, and that he had composed a "treatise I previously intended to publish," but that some authorities "have an interest in my refraining from publishing the principle of the philosophy I use." Some readers might be "shocked" by his physics. Still, "I do not apologize for their novelty."

With the help of Mersenne, the *Discourse* was widely circulated. In 1637, the year that it was published, Isaac Beeckman died. It was he who had first invited Descartes into the mathematical and mechanistic "Kingdom of science," and though their friendship had long since cooled, Descartes had called him "the one person who has shaken me out of my nonchalance." Shortly before his death, Beeckman wrote Descartes to report that a friend of his had mentioned that Descartes's "therefore I exist" sounded a lot like Augustine's *City of God*. Descartes rushed to the Leiden library to see for himself. But he conceded only that Augustine was "somewhat similar," and had been aiming to explain the Trinity. "I use it to show that this *I* which thinks is an *immaterial substance* and that there is nothing corporeal about it. These are two very different things." The distinction is important for defining Descartes's unique contribution to the debate about the soul. Others had also said that the "I" can refute skepticism, but only Descartes claimed that the "I" is a "thinking substance," an immaterial entity. The "I," he explains in the *Discourse*, "is entirely distinct from the body, and indeed is easier to know than the body, and would not fail to be whatever it is, even if the body did not exist."

With *Discourse* done, Descartes turned to his next work. With it, he was hoping to win the support of the French theological authorities, namely the Sorbonne. If he had the now-venerable institution behind him, he could move toward disclosing his scientific system. What the Sorbonne needed was a metaphysical work. It was delicate territory. He wrote in Latin to avoid stirring up a public controversy. The work began with a respectful letter to the Sorbonne theologians, and a lengthy title: *Meditations on First Philosophy In Which the Existence of God and the Distinction between the Soul and the Body are Demonstrated.*

In the *Meditations*, Descartes took his readers on a tour of the mind at once deeply introspective and deeply rational. He set out to explore the realm of pure thought, beyond the physical senses. He proved an encouraging guide. He first argued that the senses, after all, could be entirely deceptive. Dreams and instances of insanity suggested that the mind could not always tell what was real. Descartes proposed the ultimate deception. Imagine, he said, that "some malicious demon of the utmost power and cunning has employed all his energies in order to deceive me. I shall think that the sky, the air, the earth, colours, shapes, sounds, and all external things are merely delusions of dreams which he has devised to ensnare my judgement."

The idea of the devil deceiving the mind was common enough in medieval philosophy, but Descartes had given it a new twist with his imaginary demon.

Even the malicious demon, he said, cannot deceive the "thinking thing" about the act of thinking itself. So far, the *Meditations* had simply expanded on the solution to skepticism in *Discourse*. The *Discourse* had offered a proof of God from "causes," and Descartes repeated that argument in the Third Meditation (of six), insisting that the idea of God "cannot come from nothing." In the Fifth Meditation, however, he presented an authentic Ontological Proof:

> Existence can no more be separated from the essence of God than the fact that its three angles equal to two right angles can be separated from the essence of a triangle, or that the idea of a mountain can be separated from the idea of a valley.... [F]rom the fact that I cannot think of God except as existing, it follows that existence is inseparable from God, and hence that he really exists.

The mind could indeed think of fanciful things, but these things belong to a different class than that of the perfect being—as Anselm had told Gaunilo some six hundred years before. While Anselm and Descartes both had secondary ways to argue the logical necessity of God—Anselm by asserting an ultimate goodness and Descartes by saying the idea of God could not come from a finite mind—they were united in the assertion that God's essence is to exist: that is, existence is one of God's perfect attributes. As Descartes said, "For I am not free to think of God without existence (that is, a supremely perfect being without a supreme perfection) as I am free to imagine a horse with or without wings." Thinking about God, Descartes continued, was different from thinking about horses, real or fanciful, or any other imperfect being.

The *Meditations* was written in happy days with Helene and Francine, first on the coast and then in a castle near Leiden (after a move in April 1640). Then came an event all too imaginable for parents of the time: scarlet fever. It came around as often as the modern-day flu, and it took the life of five-year-old Francine in October. After this, we hear no more of Helene until Descartes vouches for her upon her first marriage, and later, when she is widowed, he again gives good wishes for her second, a happy marriage by all accounts. His family life having dissolved, Descartes stayed on in the Leiden castle for a few more months.

Soon after he left Leiden, the *Meditations* was published in France. Descartes had been innovative in soliciting comments from other thinkers to be published with the book. When the first edition came out in August 1641, it contained an appendix titled, *various objections of learned men in the demonstrations about God and the soul, together with the author's replies.* The "objections" came from such prominent men as Thomas Hobbes, the priest Pierre Gassendi, the orthodox Catholic intellectual and lawyer Antoine Arnauld, and Mersenne, who helped organize the project. The main topic was Descartes's proofs of God, and the responses were caustically critical—a fact of which Descartes took advantage by offering caustic defenses.

Descartes was again the bachelor and recluse. He moved back to the coast, this time to Endegeest, only a day's travel from The Hague, and with canal connections to Utrecht, Rotterdam, and Amsterdam. The setting was pleasant enough. He had domestic servants, a garden, and a view of fields and church towers. As he continued to grind glasses and dissect animals, Descartes dreamed that the French Jesuits would embrace his ideas in place of the old scholastic system. On the eve of the book's publication, Descartes spoke of going "to war" with them, in hopes of provoking a response, either positive or negative.

But the attention he received did not come from France, at least not from the Jesuits. The two controversies that the book engendered were focused on one particular set of responses in the *Meditations*, and on a reaction brewing among Dutch theologians to Descartes's philosophy in general. Gassendi's response to Descartes's manuscript was the longest and most critical. But he had not known that Descartes planned to publish the response, and certainly did not expect that it would be accompanied by Descartes's own published "replies." The fact that Gassendi, a mid-level church official for most of his life, was another of Mersenne's many intellectual protégés did nothing to defuse the feud that arose between Gassendi and Descartes. Gassendi, just four years older than Descartes, had ample financial encouragement from counts and nobles—patrons that Descartes lacked. This access to funds had allowed Gassendi to experiment in chemistry, be the first to see a planet (Mars) cross the sun, and commission the first map of the moon. Orthodox enough in church dogma, Gassendi was no amateur in science.

The sharp exchange that ensued between Gassendi and Descartes reveals an intellectual chasm running through the seventeenth century. They often talked past each other. But each outlined one of two great systems of thought: the metaphysical view of Anselm and Descartes, and the nominalist view of Ockham and his heirs. Though they disagreed on how universal mechanics worked—Gassendi had atoms in empty space, while Descartes postulated the "extension" of matter everywhere—their chief dispute was over the certainty of knowledge. Gassendi insisted that although individual things can be known, the extremely complex relations among things are known only vaguely, or with probabilistic knowledge (as in statistics). When it comes to God, he said, humans take a leap of faith. For Gassendi, God's power is "voluntaristic"—free and arbitrary as befits an Almighty Creator—and indeed determines the individual fate of every one of an infinite number of atoms.

Gassendi's argument is easily recognized as a page torn from Ockham. First he rejected universals: He said that there is "no universality outside of thoughts and names" and that "all universality lies in the domain of concepts or words." As he elaborated, "men do not know the inner nature of things, or their so-called real essences." Here, of course, Gassendi was addressing more than a thousand years of philosophical tradition, in which "things" and actions in the world were believed to have deep essences such as humanness, tree-ness, chairness, truthfulness, beauty, and goodness. For Gassendi, however, essences were verbal make-believe. The only knowable reality was a man, a tree, a chair, and things that people (or God) called true, beautiful, and good. As he defined reality, there were no groups of things with common natures, for "all the things which are in the world and which are able to strike the senses are singulars."

Gassendi's rebuttal to Descartes's proof would echo down through the next several centuries. He said that perfection did not logically entail "existence." "You place existence among the Divine perfections," Gassendi said to Descartes. But "existence is a perfection neither in God nor in anything else." Therefore, the argument from perfection to existence that Descartes had articulated did not work, and the use of the Platonic triangle as an illustration was not appropriate. (We can almost hear Gaunilo warning Anselm that *he* might look the fool.)

Descartes replied that God is a completely different object from anything else, even an eternal triangle. As a philosopher, of course, Descartes had to play both sides often enough. He used a triangle to exemplify an

eternal rational concept in the mind that was as irrefut-
able as the rational concept of God's existence. But on
the other hand, only God has "necessary existence," as
Anselm might have put it as well: "Hence the existence
of a triangle cannot be compared with the existence of
God, because existence manifestly has a different relation to essence in the case of God and in the case of a
triangle," he wrote to Gassendi.

The two were masters of sarcasm. Poking fun at
his rationalism and metaphysics, Gassendi addressed
Descartes as "Oh, Mind," and spoke of his "splendid
Platonic things." Descartes replied to Gassendi, the
nominalist, as "Oh, Flesh." At one point, Gassendi com-
plained that Descartes could not only describe him as
flesh, "but even as Stone, Lead, etc. or anything you
think is more obtuse."

DESPITE Descartes's success in soliciting so many
lively "objections and replies," the *Meditations* was a
publishing failure in Paris: it sold poorly and its pages
were rife with typographical errors. The Sorbonne gave
no stamp of approval. So in Holland, Descartes oversaw a new edition, published in Leiden in January 1642.
This version would finally gain Descartes the attention
he had sought, but that attention arose from a controversy with the Dutch Calvinists.

Descartes had lived in United Provinces, at that
time the most religiously tolerant place in Europe,
for more than a decade when his first writings, the

Discourse and *Essays*, were published. However, the area was also heavily Calvinist, and the Cartesian system offended Calvinist theologians, mainly because Descartes refused to use the scholastic categories and terms that even they relied upon.

A Dutch scholar, Henricus Regius, became the first to bring Cartesian philosophy to the classroom. Descartes had advised him to avoid controversy by simply flattering orthodox Calvinists and quietly teaching the "new" system. In 1640, however, Regius had become a little too bold in promoting Cartesianism. In reaction, strict Calvinists began to decry Regius and his mentor, spreading word that Descartes "lacks all modesty, is proud, supercilious, scandalous and quarrelsome." The "masked," furtive Descartes, always reluctant to enter public battle, now had to defend himself. "All I ask for is peace," he confided to an ally, "but I see that, to obtain it, I have to wage war a little."

Descartes also managed to offend Gisbertus Voetius, a famous Calvinist theologian in Utrecht. When Descartes published the 1642 *Meditations*, he had added more replies to the appendix, including one by Voetius, rector of Utrecht University. Voetius had written a letter to Mersenne on the subject of Descartes's work, and when Mersenne passed it on, Descartes was quick to publish it—and his response—in the book.

Now Voetius would get even. He conspired with another Calvinist author to issue a book that anonymously presented his scathing riposte to Descartes.

The book, sarcastically titled *The Admirable Method*, promulgated the rumor that Descartes was actually an atheist, for his proof of God was so spineless that it actually promoted disbelief. Indeed, Voetius (through his coauthor) called Descartes a "lying biped," and "king of the Cretans," no better than the heretic Lucilio Vanini, the Italian priest who had been burned in Toulouse, France, in 1619 for blasphemy, atheism, and "other crimes."

Voetius made some fair points. At the time, Calvinism and Catholicism were debating between them whether faith or reason was the path to God. A central tenet of the Protestant movement was Martin Luther's decree of "salvation by faith alone." The Cartesian rational "certainty" of God seemed excessive. Descartes began to strategize a response in his correspondence with friends. The Jesuits in France still had not noticed his work. Maybe a clash with the Calvinists, like a smoke signal to the north, wouldn't hurt. In May 1643, Descartes issued a two-hundred-page rebuttal to *The Admirable Method*. The dispute quickly boiled up, attracting attention throughout the United Provinces. Charges of slander were exchanged. In June, Descartes was summoned before the City Council in Utrecht, where Voetius lived.

The United Provinces at the time were trying to establish a balance between the powers of church and state. In that spirit, the Utrecht City Council urged both sides to retract their slander. Descartes defended himself under the principle of "religious liberty" and relied on the fact that Holland, where he lived, did not take kindly to interference from other provinces. The strategy worked, and nothing came of the suits but some welcome publicity. Descartes was becoming known for his proofs of God.

AMID all the hubbub, Descartes had completed a third work, a work that was supposed to be his grand summary. He called it *The Principles of Philosophy*. This one, he hoped, would finally win the attention of the French Jesuits, who, if they only read it, would surely receive it as the new textbook of the age.

What Descartes wanted to present was a single, unified vision of knowledge. If nominalism broke the universe into things, atoms, and probabilities, then he reconnected the parts through the certainty of the mind, and a knowable God. In the opening of the *Principles*, he presented his vision as a literal organic whole: "Thus the whole of philosophy is like a tree. The roots are metaphysics, the trunk is physics, and the branches emerging from the trunk are all the sciences, which may be reduced to three principal ones, namely medicine, mechanics and morals."

While Descartes devoted most of the *Principles* to physical science, he began with the "roots." In the first and longest of the four parts, "Principles of Human Knowledge," he explained his principles of knowledge and briefly restated his two proofs of God, this time placing the Ontological Proof first and elaborating on both. His discussion of "certainty" at the outset opened the way for his own conclusion: How certain was he of his own philosophy and physics? For Descartes, there were degrees of certainty, God's existence being most certain, and everyday moral judgments, based on experience and wisdom, least. He was careful in how he presented his findings, far more careful than Galileo had been. Perhaps it was for insurance against heresy that he introduced the idea that the mind could know two kinds of objects, either "things" or "eternal truths." Whenever he spoke of physical science, he clarified, he was not speaking of "eternal truths" but of "things." Nothing, however, could stop him from hoping that eventually "these results of mine will be allowed in the class of absolute certainties," the realm of mathematics, reason, and metaphysics. For the time being, he submitted "all these opinions to the authority of the Catholic Church and the judgment of those wiser than myself."

After sixteen years away from France, Descartes planned to make a triumphant return home for the publication of the *Principles*. He left Holland in the summer of 1644, before the books were even printed, sailing from Amsterdam to Calais. Then he headed overland to Paris. As the June sun beat down, and as he passed by so many familiar sights—haystacks, church steeples, and peasants in grey—Descartes realized how much his native France had changed. The great Cardinal Richelieu was dead. England was embroiled in a Puritan civil war, and both skeptic and Catholic-leaning Englishmen had fled to France.

Back in Amsterdam, several copies of the *Principles* rolled off the presses in July. Descartes passed through Paris quickly, and as he rode south intending to attend to some family business, a shipment of his books reached purveyors in the city. Descartes got in touch with a former rector of La Flèche, claiming—disingenuously—that the *Principles* was "innocent" of dangerous innovation and indeed abided by "the views that are taught in the Schools." He visited other Jesuits, passed around a dozen copies of the *Principles*, and hurried back north, obviously preferring the life of a recluse in a small coastal village of Holland.

Descartes's triumphal return of 1644 was no triumph at all. The Jesuits idly thumbed his book's pages: a few wrote inoffensive letters. But the intellectual coup that Descartes had expected didn't happen. Back home, Descartes wrote a friend: "I have got 20 years older than I was last year." The footloose philosopher was slowing down. Travel had become harder. He was nearly fifty, and now seen always in the black wig he had ordered from Paris, both to hide his gray hair and to stay warm in the cold north.

He had moved to Egmond, a seaside "hermitage" in Holland, where he would finish out his long residency in the Netherlands, as that region is called today. He continued writing letters to Jesuits in France, keeping after them to use *Principles*, but Descartes had grown weary of public debate. At Egmond he culti-vated plants instead of reading books. When a visitor watched him dissect a calf as part of his anatomical research, Descartes pointed to the bloody remains: "This is my library!"

To some, Descartes seemed a curmudgeon, over-sensitive about his ideas and his place in history. He had not become a complete recluse, however. In Holland, he attended Mass quietly, but also visited Calvinist churches with friends and went to hear Anabaptist sermons. Certain rumors never went away, especially after the battle with Voetius. As he told Mersenne, "the Huguenots hate me as a papist, and those of Rome do not like me because they think I am entangled in the heresy of the Earth's movement." Still, the Netherlands was the freest realm he knew.

PRINCESS Elisabeth of Bohemia was an infant in Prague when Descartes was a soldier and her father, King Frederick, fled to The Hague after his army's defeat in 1620. The princess, who still lived in Holland, knew the scholar Henricus Regius, and at his recom-mendation had read the *Meditations*. In May 1643, at the height of the Voetius dispute, Descartes received a letter from her, full of questions about his argument. Always pragmatic, Descartes persuaded Elisabeth to lend her name as royal sponsor of the *Principles*, which gave the book credibility and immunity from censor-ship; he wrote the dedication to her "Serene Highness."

They carried on a lively correspondence, in which
Descartes freely explored his mechanistic view of animals and humans, an area of controversy that he had
withheld from discussing in his latest work. "I will try
here to explain the manner in which I conceive of the
union of the soul with the body and how the soul has
the power [*force*] to move it," he said in his first reply
to Elisabeth. By presenting the mind as a different substance from matter, Descartes set up a "dualism" that
he had to justify for the rest of his days, especially as he
turned his attention to anatomy.

Descartes's and Elisabeth's mutual enjoyment of
their correspondence is evident in the fifty-nine letters
they exchanged over the course of seven years. On occasion, he would travel to The Hague to see her in person.
Even after family troubles forced her to flee to Berlin in
the final years of the Thirty Years War, they continued
to write. Elisabeth was not too emphatic on the point
of her higher social rank, often coyly presenting herself as an "ignorant and intractable person" before the
career philosopher. Descartes in turn spoke of himself
as a "very humble and obedient servant."

Elisabeth had a keen mind and loved to point out
contradictions. If, for example, Descartes's physics said
motion requires contact, how does the brain make matter move if they are separate substances? Furthermore,
in Descartes's theory of animal spirits, or fine matter
circulating in the blood, how do those spirits touch

matter? Her first letter asked "how the soul of a human being (it being only a thinking substance) can determine the bodily [animal] spirits, in order to bring about voluntary actions?" It was a puzzle for her young mind: "This is why I ask you for a more precise definition of the soul than the one you give in your *Metaphysics*."

DESCARTES's responses were his first genuine attempt to speculate about how the human mind and body *interact*. His reply was as usual: mind was a distinct substance, and matter only an extension. Elisabeth wasn't satisfied. She presented the position of Thomas Hobbes: mind was simply an excretion of brute matter. In Descartes's correspondence with Hobbes, with whom he'd had short but stormy exchanges, he argued that science had not yet proved whether the mind was material or immaterial, so it was best to "apply different names to those substances that we recognize as the subjects of completely different acts"—in other words, the mind was still best thought of as a "thinking substance."

To satisfy Elisabeth, Descartes urged her to consider the mind-body relationship in two different ways: as an interaction, but also as separated and distinct realities. The discussion finally prompted him to write yet another work, a feeble effort at best, to explain to Elisabeth what was perhaps inexplicable. He called it *A Treatise on the Passions of the Soul*. Descartes had gotten canny when it came to the business of publishing. He

commented that *Passions of the Soul* might not "do any
better" than his other treatises, though "its title may
possibly attract more people to read it."

In the entire work, how the soul makes contact
with the body comes up only once, when Descartes
repeats his theory that the "soul has its principal seat
in the small gland located in the middle of the brain"—
the pineal gland. *The Passions of the Soul* spent more
time on other topics in his correspondence with
Elisabeth, which ought to be clear from the book's
title: passions, the will, virtue, moods. Once, when she
was ill, he suggested a psychosomatic cause: troubled
emotions affecting her health. These were the conun-
drums of the *Passions of the Soul*. Just how did mood
and imagination affect the blood? The *Passions of the
Soul* was a return to the biological vision Descartes had
hinted at fifteen years earlier in *The World*: the animal
spirits, which carried moods and intentions, moved
through nerves as fine matter through tubes, carrying
the "will" that moves muscles. This organic connection
developed after birth, preserving Descartes's idea of
mind as a separate "thinking substance."

In 1648, the Thirty Years War drew to a close.
Between April and June, the cities of the new Dutch
republic lit up with parades, bonfires, fireworks,
pageants, thanksgiving services, open-air theater, and
sumptuous banquets for militia and civic leaders.
For the United Provinces, the Peace of Munster also
meant the end of its near-century-long struggle to

become independent of Spain. It was in that conflict that Descartes had found early employment as a border sentry. The present political shift forced him to consider where he would live out the rest of his days. Amid the celebrations in Holland, he set off for Paris totally unaware of what was to come: a revolt of the nobility against the French crown.

When Descartes arrived in Paris, the revolt was just brewing. The tension between the nobility and the crown began to escalate over higher taxes, and members of Parliament also felt threatened when the king and his chief minister, Cardinal Jules Mazarin, arrested one of its own on charges of being a rabble-rouser. Between 1648 and 1653, the nobility tried to take arms against the royal household, an aborted uprising called the *Fronde*, French for "sling," and the name of the opposition party as well. Descartes could not have been less interested. He visited Mersenne and had two friendly meetings with his old rival Gassendi, friends at least in their revolt against Aristotle.

The populace took the side of Parliament, and when the crown started making arrests, the streets exploded. On August 26, 1648, mobs set up barricades and engaged the royal troops, just back from the Thirty Years War, so the king and his family fled. On the next day, August 27, Descartes packed and escaped to his coastal hermitage in Holland. But even Holland no longer seemed safe. Mersenne had died soon after his visit: Descartes's most important tie to the outside world was now gone. By January 1649, the Cromwellian rebellion in England had beheaded the Catholic-leaning King Charles I, Princess Elizabeth's uncle. In a February 22 letter, Descartes sent her condolences on the "fatal conclusion of the tragedies of England," noting further that it was more glorious to die in public than in one's bed, an old sentiment from his soldiering days.

Just about that time, Descartes's old friend Pierre Chanut, a French diplomat formerly posted in the Netherlands, contacted him with a proposal. Chanut was now in Sweden and had shared Descartes's works with Christina, the Queen of Sweden. Thus was born the idea of a French philosopher at the court. Chanut extended the invitation. At the time, Descartes's critics seemed formidable. Even Holland was mounting an Inquisition. He needed a protector of "power and virtue"—young Elisabeth, herself in exile, was not enough. Though neither France nor the United Provinces had recognized his accomplishments, now a queen called. Descartes settled his debts and assigned his papers to an executor. He finally left in 1649, joking in his last letter from Holland that he might well die in a shipwreck. Friends gathered for a farewell, and a local painter dashed off his portrait. Then Descartes and his valet sailed out of the harbor of Amsterdam, crossed the North Sea, and arrived in Stockholm in October.

Right away, he regretted his decision. He wrote to Elisabeth that he worried over the queen's ability to learn philosophy, seriously doubting that he would "be capable of giving her any satisfaction or of being in any way useful to her." The queen, evidently intuiting something of his discontent, offered him inducements to stay: a noble title and a reduction of his duties to a single morning philosophy lesson (since Descartes found the court frivolity repugnant). But for Descartes, an inveterate late sleeper, work that early was torture.

He had a few consolations. In November, he learned that the *Passions*, written in French, had been published in both Amsterdam and Paris. Then the Swedish winter descended. His depression deepened. The court viewed him as a foreign Catholic interloper, a worrisome influence on the young Lutheran queen. Descartes wrote to Chanut, "I am not in my element here." Not even "the most powerful kings on earth" can give peace and contentment, he concluded. He was living at the French ambassador's home when, in early February, he caught a flu that was going around and was bedridden for days on end, fighting a fever. After eight days he sank into unconsciousness. Descartes died in the early hours of February 11, 1650, just shy of his fifty-fourth birthday.

His biographers report that it was a beautiful passing: the philosopher was surrounded by friends, the court, and a priest to administer his final confession and last rites. Across Europe, the news was received with sadness, and Descartes's admirers honored him with epitaphs and memorials. The famous Dutch physicist, Christian Huygens (son of the statesman), wrote

in French, "O, Nature mourn…The Great Descartes."
In another poem, Chanut recalled Descartes's youthful
journeys:

> …on his way to the army
> amid the calm of winter
> combining nature's mysteries with the laws of
> mathesis,
> dared to hope,
> with one single key, to unlock the secrets of both.

The funeral came two days later, in accordance
with Catholic rites. The ambassador's staff carried the
coffin. There were few mourners when it was laid in the
cemetery at the orphan's hospital, a cemetery for non-
Christians—Sweden was a Protestant country—and
victims of plague. Chanut took up the task of organizing Descartes's papers, including his seven-year correspondence with Elizabeth. She quickly sent a messenger to confiscate them. Their discussion of "passions"
could easily have been misunderstood.

Ten years later, France finally began to notice
Descartes. So did the Roman Church. He had spent a
lifetime trying not to offend the decrees of Trent, but in
1663, exactly thirty years after he personally suppressed
The World, his great work on the mechanistic universe, his writings were put on the Index of Forbidden
Books. As with Lanfranc and Berengar in the eleventh
century, and Ockham in the fourteenth, Descartes

had stumbled on the doctrine of the Eucharist, which stipulated that any tampering with Aristotelian physics violated church dogma: Christ had a "real presence" as Aristotelian substance in bread, whether it was baked in France, England, or Holland.

In a literal manifestation of his posthumous fame, France brought Descartes home. Exhumed from his grave of sixteen years, his remains were put in a new coffin for travel. After a journey by land and sea, including a three-month delay at customs, his body arrived in Paris in 1667. The coffin was temporarily placed in Saint Paul's Church, then moved to Saint Genevieve de Mont—but not permanently: Descartes's bones were shuttled around by the political winds (and his finger and skull were reportedly taken as souvenirs). The politics stirred by the French Revolution almost landed him in the Pantheon, but he was finally laid to rest in 1819 in the former Benedictine monastery at Saint-Germain Des Prés.

By then, Descartes's ideas had become a popular topic in the Paris salons. His letters and manuscripts were already being published in several languages, and what remained of *The World* was finally set into type in 1664. In the brief span of fifteen years, Cartesian philosophy had become a crucial element in the history of Western thought. Descartes stood for the modern philosophical project. He rejected received opinion and marked the transition to a new empiricism. He built a system from scratch, hoping it could persuade the Turk,

Christian, and skeptic alike. He was emphatic that there was a place for theology within a materialist universe. In the end, certainty about the self and God led to certainty about a rational universe studied by science. His physics was naive, but the body of his work virtually defines the range of our modern questions about knowledge, subjectivity, consciousness, the nature of science, matter, and even reality. He also brought the Ontological Proof of God into the modern world.

CHAPTER 9

The Ontological Proof

TRINITY Lane winds through Cambridge University like a cobblestoned alley, past orderly corridors of street lamps and row houses with narrow chimneys. The old shops on the lane are now gone, but not much else has changed since 1894, when a young Bertrand Russell—one of the greatest logical minds of the twentieth century—passed that way, threw his tobacco tin in the air, caught it, and exclaimed "Great Scott, the ontological argument is sound!" As he recalled years later, "I saw in a flash (or thought I saw) that the ontological argument is valid."

Russell was born in 1872, heir to a British family of lords, freethinkers, and Puritans. He sidestepped a career in English politics to study philosophy and mathematics at Cambridge. Well after his idealistic student days, when proofs of God had fleetingly caught his fancy, Russell coproduced the era's magnum opus on mathematical logic, the *Principia Mathematica* (1910–1913). Ensconced at Cambridge, he became a leading skeptic, materialist, and pacifist. Among his many achievements, including winning a Nobel Prize in literature, Russell popularized philosophy in general, and threw new light on the Ontological Argument.

Like Trinity Lane, the Ontological Argument had walked a zigzag path. It has been reinvented, challenged, revived, and declared defeated. Russell said years later, "Modern logic has proved this argument invalid," but "it is easier to feel convinced that it must be fallacious than it is to find out precisely where the fallacy lies."

After Descartes, the searches for both proof and fallacy continued. In the twentieth century, the work of Russell and his colleagues revived the great nominalist worldview. Ockham's ideas were godless in this new iteration—but no less insistent in the quest to reduce all reality to material objects. Between Descartes's grand unity and Russell's new nominalism, this enduring divide manifested itself once again.

On the European continent, the rationalists had taken Descartes's lead, at least in eschewing skepticism and looking for a system that would unify God and the world. The two earliest converts to the Cartesian approach were the Dutch philosopher Baruch Spinoza and the German philosopher Gottfried Leibniz. Spinoza, who viewed God and the universe as one material continuum (a doctrine called pantheism), used the Ontological Argument to argue that God was necessary, whereas Leibniz elaborated on Descartes by adding, "assuming that God is possible, he exists." Leibniz boasted that it was he who persuaded Spinoza of this truth: "I showed this reasoning to D. Spinoza when I was in The Hague, who thought it solid; for when at first he opposed it, I put it in writing and read this paper before him."

As this pro-Ontological Proof trend gained ground in Europe, the nominalists gained ground in Britain, led by the Scottish philosopher and skeptic David Hume. His interpretation of nominalism followed in the footsteps of Ockham and Gassendi. Hume went further, seeming to reject outright a belief in God. He argued that no cause can be proved for anything: one is only habituated to such "truths" as the idea that the sun will rise tomorrow. If that could not be proved, then certainly an ineffable divine cause was the hardest of all to prove.

In chapter nine of Hume's *Dialogues Concerning Natural Religion*, the three protagonists debate the very premise of the Ontological Proof: that is, whether anything can have "necessary existence." The character representing Hume's viewpoint calls necessary existence "absurd," for nothing is necessary: "Whatever we conceive as existent, we can also conceive as nonexistent. There is no Being, therefore, whose nonexistence implies a contradiction. Consequently there is no Being, whose existence is demonstrable."

Hume's skepticism about "causes" also traveled to the northern edges of Germany. In the city of Koningsberg, it influenced Immanuel Kant, the leather strap-maker's son turned professor. Kant—who between the American and French Revolutions had declared an "age of enlightenment"—at first was inspired by the continental rationalism spawned by the Cartesians. But he finally decided against Descartes and

Leibniz, and in his *Critique of Pure Reason*, offered his famous chapter "On the Impossibility of an Ontological Proof of the Existence of God." The chapter gave the Anselmian debate its modern title: "the Ontological Proof," *ontology* being a Greek term for "the study of being" that had just entered European philosophy.

Kant also handed down for the ages an argument and slogan that, while asserted already by Gassendi and Hume, would eventually become a classic slogan of Kantianism: "Existence is not a predicate." Both Anselm and Descartes had relied on the syllogism that one of God's perfections (subject) was existence (predicate). The syllogism went thus:

> God is the being with all the perfections.
> Existence is a perfection.
> Therefore, God possesses existence.

Hume summed up the nominalist protest nicely when he said, "To reflect on any thing simply, and to reflect on it as existent, are nothing different from each other." The idea of existence, in other words, had no role in logic. Things just existed; that was all. Kant offered an example concerning the value of a hundred thalers, or dollars, in his pocket: "A hundred real thalers do not contain the least coin more than a hundred possible thalers."

In the nineteenth century, the German philosopher George W. F. Hegel took up the Ontological

Argument, at least according to what we know from the notes of his students. Hegel proposed that culture and ideas evolved dialectically—one can think of this as a sort of "call and response." Any idea proposed is quickly contradicted by another, and the debate between the two resolves itself into a better idea, at which point the process begins again. Hegel's contention was that through the course of history, this "dialectic" process moves humanity closer and closer to perfection, or the Absolute. The Hegelian system was called Absolute Idealism, with the Absolute usually standing for God. When it came to an Ontological Proof of the Absolute, Hegel seemed to say that the whole must come before the parts, the Absolute must exist before the dialectic of things and ideas—hence, God exists. Hegel's new breed of ontology would eventually supercede Kant's *Critique* in the philosophy departments of British universities, especially at Cambridge, which had nurtured the young Bertrand Russell.

As a graduate student at Cambridge, Russell had been persuaded of the Ontological Argument by his teacher, the leading Absolute Idealist of British philosophy, Francis H. Bradley. As Bradley once said, "What may be and must be, is." This was the secular Ontological Argument in its purest form. "When I was young," Russell later wrote, "I hoped to find religious satisfaction in philosophy; even after I had abandoned Hegel, the eternal Platonic world [of Descartes and mathematics] gave me something nonhuman to admire."

Later in life, Russell gave up his early romance with cosmic unity and replaced it with what he came to call the philosophy of logical analysis (also known as "logical positivism"). He described history as a battle between the "mathematical party," to which Plato, Anselm, and Descartes belonged, and the empiricists, typified by Ockham, Hume, and others. The empirical party was on the right path. The world, Russell proposed, was made up of a number of simple facts, each independent, but related. He tried to reduce both mathematics and logic to a perfect language that would enable us to talk about this world. This simple language would function as an absolutely "minimum vocabulary," as he put it. "It is here that I have found Occam's razor useful."

Logical analysis dominated Anglo-American philosophy for most of the twentieth century. It cast aside all metaphysical inquiry. In time, as with so many philosophical systems, it would suffer the same fate. Along with Russell, the Austrian philosopher Ludwig Wittgenstein had been a key player in initiating the movement of logical analysis, but ironically it was Wittgenstein who also brought about its downfall. It turned out that logical analysis itself could not be verified to the philosophers' satisfaction, and its nominalist quest to identify all "things" with simple words proved futile. Finally, the new logicians had to concede that no complex system, mathematical or otherwise, could be entirely logically consistent. Russell was caught in the lurch, but as usual, took the new intellectual crisis philosophically. One of his favorite terms for assessing past philosophical failures was "antiquated" philosophy. In the wake of Wittgenstein's razor, so to speak, Russell was forced to apply the term to himself: "It is not an altogether pleasant experience to find oneself regarded as antiquated after having been, for a time, in fashion."

One element of that fashion, at least, had endured: the philosophical debate over words. The early thrust of logical analysis focused on grammar. Words had to attach themselves to clear things, which could also be thought of as "pictures" of a situation. Wittgenstein argued that the only world that human beings truly know is the one created by the manipulation of words themselves. Reality was found in the rules of grammar and semantics, or what he called "language-games." That was the main point of his posthumously published *Philosophical Investigations* (1953). Each human group invented its own language game. Ordinary language, of course, identifies ordinary things, and Wittgenstein did not deny that fact. But when it came to complex ideas and interpretations of life, all that could be said was: "This language-game is played." Therefore, he concluded, philosophy had no real problems, such as proofs of God, but instead only puzzles of language.

Russell was never quite convinced that language games are the only reality. Although he failed in his vision of a "new logic" and a final "theory of descriptions" of all things, he still wished to preserve logical analysis, coupled with scientific experiment, as the surest way to knowledge:

> I do not myself believe that philosophy can either prove or disprove the truth of religious dogmas, but ever since Plato most philosophers have considered it part of their business to produce 'proofs' of immortality and the existence of God. They have found fault with the proofs of their predecessors—Saint Thomas rejected Saint Anselm's proofs, and Kant rejected Descartes'—but they have supplied new ones of their own. In order to make their proofs seem valid, they have had to falsify logic, to make mathematics mystical, and to pretend that deep-seated prejudices were heaven-sent intuitions. All this is rejected by the philosophers who make logical analysis the main business of philosophy.

NEAR the end of his career, Russell undertook a massive project, entitled simply *A History of Western Philosophy*. It was 1945, the world had just begun recovering from the Second World War, and a depressed Russell was living in the United States despite the fact that his appointment at City College in New York had been revoked some years earlier due to widespread public protests. He was as surprised as his publisher when his huge tome became an immediate best seller.

The book's popularity stemmed from a new way of viewing philosophy as an expression of both political and economic interests, as well as an intellectual pursuit, however naive, of "pure" truth, such as proof of God. Russell surveyed the centuries with his benign gaze, acknowledging Anselm of Canterbury for his boldness in finding God "in the mind," applauding Descartes for his "freshness" as a "discoverer and explorer," but ultimately favoring Ockham, whom he ranked as "the most important schoolman" after Thomas Aquinas. Before Ockham, logic and philosophy had been taken over by metaphysics and theology. Ockham had separated them again: "By insisting on the possibility of studying logic and human knowledge without reference to metaphysics and theology, Occam's work encouraged scientific research."

Russell declared that the Ontological Argument was both wrong and irrelevant, an archaic form of metaphysics; but he gave credit to Anselm and Descartes. Anselm, he explained, had championed the notion that a thought, by its very activity, can prove that something outside the mind truly exists. Russell joked that philosophers, who trafficked only in ideas and thoughts, have always yearned for ideas to turn into real things that the world had to recognize. Either way, Anselm had presented one of these great ideas in "its naked logical purity," Russell said, and posterity—or at least the philosophers of subsequent eras—did indeed have to deal with it. "Clearly an argument with such a distinguished history is to be treated with respect, whether valid or not," Russell concluded.

In the final analysis, the Ontological Proof is a form of logic that appeals to reason. This logic is organized around a premise, which tries to persuade everyone that it is self-evident or necessary, or at the very least useful. When everyone agrees that all men are mortal, for example, it becomes universally "valid" to say that an individual like Socrates is mortal. However, much of philosophy and science is based on premises that are not universally accepted. Similarly, the Ontological Proof operates on the premise that there is a "greatest" reality. Nowadays, those who accept this premise as self-evident, necessary, or useful, would say the Ontological Proof is at least logically "valid." In technical philosophy, however, it hardly is proof positive of God's existence. As the Cambridge philosopher Jonathan Barnes summarized in 1972: "There is no reason to accept it as proof of theism, since there is no reason to believe a presupposition of its first premiss, namely the proposition that there is just one thing than which nothing greater can be imagined."

Epilogue

TODAY, the idea of 'proof' makes more sense in mathematical disciplines, courtrooms, and scientific testing than it does in relation to the existence of God. But the modern mind still thirsts for some kind of proof that God exists—or the opposite. When it comes to proofs, scientific or philosophical, those based on external evidence have always been easier to accept. Science bases its claims on the measurement and testing of external evidence. These so-called scientific proofs, grounded in the world of our experience, have enjoyed prominence since Aristotle.

When Aristotle was rediscovered in the West, Thomas Aquinas used his approach to put forth "five ways" in which the existence of God could be pondered: 1) motion suggests a first mover; 2) causes suggest a first cause; 3) the contingency of things suggests a necessary source; 4) the world's gradations of less and more require an ultimate standard; and, 5) natural things have purposeful ends, so there must be an intelligent governor.

Not surprisingly, proofs of God based on physical evidence remain compelling: think, for instance, of the present controversy over "intelligent design." Even the great skeptic David Hume, who is said to have banished knowledge of all causes from the physical universe, conceded that the argument from design—that a being of intelligence and power created a world of order and direction—was not completely irrational. But as to ontological proofs, Hume maintained that these were only persuasive to people of "metaphysical head." The Ontological Proof is a proof from abstraction, which is not only hard to understand as a form of pure logic, but verges on being a world of make-believe—a plight it shares with some forms of abstract mathematics, physics, and even the "deep time" of historical biology.

By definition, the world of abstraction—the realm of questions about why and how things exist—is where the physical senses lose their influence. The mind relies instead on its powers of reason, logic, intuition, and insight. No one would deny that these powers of the mind motivate science, art, literature, education, and religion. In short, abstraction motivates human belief.

The abstraction of metaphysics might be a stretch for the average person's intellect, but words must still mean something to us all. As Russell so simply stated: "If a word means something, there must be some thing that it means." If "God" means nothing, then the debate is off. But when the question is belief and disbelief, God must take on a distinct character. Atheists and agnostics have perpetually worked to define the supernatural deity they reject. For most believers, in turn, God is more than a logical abstraction, for a God who makes a difference in the world must be a kind of *being* (or *person*) that pays attention to human affairs.

Nevertheless, in a scientific age that doubts the possibility of God's existence, even an abstract God can be a step forward, for such a God connects the mind, the world, logic, and words. Anselm referred to God as "something than which nothing greater can be thought." Though an abstract concept, this "something" of Anselm's was set apart as the ultimate cause and ultimate goodness, which by definition eliminated any rivals to the claim. It's an argument that still demands a response. Anselm set up the debate in absolute terms: does God exist or not? The fool said, "There is no God." Anselm said logic proves there is.

We're left with a few simple choices.

For disbelief: there are two compelling reasons. First, God can be judged illogical or impossible, either for rational or for moral reasons. Second—and this is the argument of positivism—only *things* are real, and God is not a thing that can be pointed at and named. While this attitude often implies disbelief, positivists can still be believers, by a leap of faith. This is the Ockhamist position, also called *fideism*—the proverbial leap of faith, a willful belief despite the lack of any physical evidence or logical necessity.

Believers have a rational option as well. This is the approach of "metaphysical realism," championed by the ancients, Anselm, and Descartes. They accepted the premise that God is the foundation of a real world "out there," and then commenced to put that world into rational order. Even today, most people believe in God; atheists are still a minority in the West. The impulse of metaphysical realism begins in the mind, where many people find God by way of their own reason, intuition, and common sense.

Lately, the debate over what is in the mind has moved to neuroscience: we use technology as Descartes used dissection, to look into the brain to see what is there. Neuroscientists cheerfully announce that they haven't found a "thinking substance," let alone God himself, in the brain. In the evolutionary view, belief in "causes" helped human survival, and now brain researchers claim to have found the very "God module" or "God gene" that drives the human propensity to believe. Others observe blood flowing through the brain to detect neurological activity that might explain the "oceanic" feeling that we call God. If the idea of "something than which nothing greater can be thought" does seem logical, neuroscience maintains that this idea is no more mysterious than mathematics, music, or beauty, all of which derive from the "things" that make up the brain—its modules, neuronal networks, and the ebb and flow of chemicals that trigger our thoughts, memories, emotions, and the five senses.

Maybe the findings of neuroscience will turn out to be true, and few are willing to challenge the objective findings of so revered a profession as science. Modern science operates on the power it inherited from nominalism, a "bottom-up" approach in which *things* are the bedrock of reality. To say that God abides in the human mind, however, has a "top-down" quality. Most people are not yet persuaded that *things* create God. For all we know, the quest of neuroscience to isolate both God and the "I," while well intended and well funded, may be as hopeless as Gaunilo's search to find the Lost Island, the most perfect island that anyone had ever seen. But that is a different search from the one that looks for a necessary, absolute, and perfect Being. Anselm's confident, or deluded, words ring down to us from nearly a millennium ago: "What, I ask, could be more logical?"

Acknowledgments

THIS book began with an idea, much in the way that the philosophers in this book began. For a writer, the question was, 'Can something as nebulous as the medieval Ontological Proof be explained in a popular book?' For encouraging this idea, I thank my agent, Giles Anderson. My wife gave unswerving support for the variously called "Anselm book," "proof book," "medieval book"—and, "Oh, the book." My thanks go to my sage editors, James Atlas and Jessica Fjeld, whose advice was indispensable, and to John Oakes, also of Atlas & Co. Most of all, I owe a debt to two professors, both of whom patiently corrected my errors: Sharon M. Kaye of John Carroll University, author of *On Ockham*, and Jorge Secada of the University of Virginia, author of *Cartesian Metaphysics: The Scholastic Origins of Modern Philosophy*. Of course, my approach in this little book is my own. I'm grateful to the many biographers and critics whose work informed my research.

Notes

THERE is no English translation of the complete works of Anselm, Ockham, or Descartes. Accordingly, I have had to assemble my quotations in a somewhat piecemeal fashion.

The primary sources of material for Anselm are two books by R. W. Southern: his translation of the *Life of St. Anselm* and his biography, *Saint Anselm: A Portrait in a Landscape*, which translates many of Anselm's letters and includes an exacting chronology. The bulk of Anselm's philosophical works are translated in Brian Davies et al., *Anselm of Canterbury: The Major Works*.

Most details of Ockham's life are lost to history; I have adhered to the conventional reconstruction. Philotheus Boehner's translated anthology, *Ockham: Philosophical Writings*, proved invaluable, as have secondary works such as Marilyn McCord Adams's *William Ockham, 2 vols*.

The nearly complete works of Descartes are compiled in French in the twelve-volume *Oeuvres de Descartes* by Charles Adam and Paul Tannery. For English translations, I have mainly relied on the three volumes of John Cottingham et al.'s *The Philosophical Writings of Descartes*, the third volume of which contains a helpful selection of letters. I made frequent use of Desmond Clarke's invaluable biography, *Descartes*, and have also quoted from translations by Stephen Gaukroger and Lisa Shapiro.

ABBREVIATIONS

ACMW   Brian Davies and G. R. Evans, eds., *Anselm of Canterbury: The Major Works* (New York: Oxford University Press, 1998).

DAB   Desmond M. Clarke, *Descartes: A Biography* (Cambridge: Cambridge University Press, 2006).

HWP   Bertrand Russell, *A History of Western Philosophy, and Its Connection with Political and Social Circumstances from the Earliest Times to the Present Day* (New York: Simon and Schuster, 1945).

LSA   Eadmer, *The Life of St Anselm: Archbishop of Canterbury*, ed. R. W. Southern (London: Thomas Nelson, 1962).

OPW   Philotheus Boehner, ed. and trans. *Ockham: Philosophical Writings* (Indianapolis: Hackett Publishing Company, 1990).

PWD   John Cottingham, Robert Stoothoff, and Dugald
1 and 2 Murdoch, eds., *The Philosophical Writings of Descartes*, 2 vols. (Cambridge: Cambridge University Press, 1984).

SAPL   R. W. Southern, *Saint Anselm: A Portrait in a Landscape* (Cambridge: Cambridge University Press, 1990).

TOA   Alvin Plantinga, ed., *The Ontological Argument: From St. Anselm to Contemporary Philosophers* (London: Macmillan, 1968).

WOW   Stephen Gaukroger, ed. and trans., *The World and Other Writings René Descartes,* (Cambridge: Cambridge University Press, 1998).

OTHER WORKS CONSULTED

John Hick and Arthur C. McGill, eds., *The Many-Faced Argument: Recent Studies on the Ontological Argument for the Existence of God* (New York: Macmillan, 1967).

Jorge Secada, *Cartesian Metaphysics: The Scholastic Origins of Modern Philosophy* (New York: Cambridge University Press, 2000).

PREFACE: ANSELM'S FOOL

p. 1 "There is no God": Psalms 13:1; 52:1.

p. 2 "something than which nothing greater can be thought": *ACMW*, 87.

p. 3 "I should find it hard to decide": *ACMW*, 109.

p. 3 "is understood and is in the mind": *ACMW*, 113.

p. 3 "an arrogant modernizer": *ACMW*, 6.

p. 8 "What Descartes has borrowed from Anselm": quoted in *TOA*, 54.

p. 9 "The famous Ontological Argument": quoted in *TOA*, 66.

p. 9 "Great Scott, the Ontological Argument": Russell in *The Philosophy of Bertrand Russell*, ed. Paul Arthur (Evanston, IL: Northwestern University Press, 1944), 10.

CHAPTER 1: THE LOGIC OF GOD

p. 15 "whitest of bread": *LSA*, 5.

p. 15 "gradually turned from study": *LSA*, 6.

p. 16 "The ship of his heart": *LSA*, 6.

p. 18 "Each Christian people strove": eleventh-century monk Raul Glaber quoted in Horst de la Croix and Richard G. Tansey, *Art Through the Ages*, 5th ed. (New York: Harcourt, 1970), 303.

p. 21 "lose the reward": *LSA*, 8.

p. 21 "Well then, I shall become a monk": *LSA*, 9.

p. 21 "So put aside your rebelliousness": *LSA*, 9.

p. 25 "And if you are ever called": *LSA*, 22.

p. 26 "sent out his pupils": quoted in *SAPL*, 17.

p. 28 "thus hiding [his] art": quoted in *SAPL*, 51.

p. 31 "It is not possible for fire": *The Complete Works of Aristotle*, vol. 1, rev. Oxford Translation, ed. and trans. Jonathan Barnes (Princeton: Princeton University Press, 1984), 20.

p. 33 "He attained such a height": *LSA*, 12.

p. 34 "I do not doubt that we both love": quoted in *SAPL*, 145.

p. 34 "I am the poorest and basest of *homunculi*": quoted in *SAPL*, 101.

p. 34 "In it, the soul of the sinner": quoted in *SAPL*, 93.

p. 35 "The purpose of the prayers and meditations": quoted in *SAPL*, 448.

p. 36 "only the pope's feet": quoted in Richard P. McBrien, *Lives of the Pope: The Pontiffs from St. Peter to John Paul II* (San Francisco: HarperSanFrancisco, 1997), 186.

CHAPTER 2: "I BEGAN TO WONDER"

p. 39 "But listen!": *ACMW*, 33.

p. 39 "Come now, insignificant man": *ACMW*, 84.

p. 40 "I did not dare to disobey": quoted in *SAPL*, 412.

p. 41 "where his interest lay": *LSA*, 28.

p. 41 "Some of my brethren have": *ACMW*, 5.

p. 41 "made up of a connected chain"; "one single argument": *ACMW*, 82.

p. 42 "Since, then, the supreme nature": *ACMW*, 30.

p. 43 "simply by reason alone": *ACMW*, 11.

p. 43 "The rational mind may be the only": *ACMW*, 72.

p. 43 "If, then, someone thinks"; "I would ask them not": *ACMW*, 6.

p. 43 "However often I look over what": quoted in *SAPL*, 71.

p. 43 "for the sake of greater convenience": *ACMW*, 83.

p. 44 "I began to wonder": *ACMW*, 82.

p. 44 "gave him great trouble": *LSA*, 29.

p. 45 "Then suddenly one night": *LSA*, 30.

p. 45 "composed a volume, small in size": *LSA*, 31.

p. 47 "Certainly this being so truly exists": *ACMW*, 88.

p. 47 "We define 'God' as the greatest possible object": *HWP*, 417.

p. 48 "So if God exists His existence is necessary": Norman Malcolm quoted in *TOA*, 146. Charles Hartshorne offers this more difficult summary of Anselm's second argument: "If God could conceivably fail to exist, He must be something which, 'even if it existed,' would be less than 'that than which none greater can be conceived'; for we can (it is claimed) conceive of something such that it cannot be conceived not to exist, and to be thus is better than to be such that the nonexistence of the thing is conceivable." See Hartshorne's *Anselm's Discovery: A Re-Examination of the Ontological Proof for God's Existence* (Chicago: Open Court, 1965), 34.

p. 48 "($\forall y$)((($\exists^x$)": Jonathan Barnes, *The Ontological Argument* (London: Macmillan Press Ltd., 1972), 88.

p. 48 "only general, non-technical": *SAPL*, 128.

p. 49 "found fault with one of"; "read it with pleasure": *LSA*, 31.

p. 49 "I can so little think of or entertain": *ACMW*, 107.

p. 49 "in my mind and not": *ACMW*, 108.

p. 50 "So much for the claim": *ACMW*, 108.

p. 51 "Surely then . . . 'that-than-which-a-greater'": *ACMW*, 113.

p. 51 "Lost Island"; "If, I say, someone wishes to thus persuade me": *ACMW*, 109.

p. 52 "For 'that which is greater than everything'": *ACMW*, 116.

p. 52 "magnitude," from Seneca's *Quaestiones Naturales*; "nothing can be imagined," from Boethius's *Consolation of Philosophy*: quoted in Julius R. Weinberg, *Ockham, Descartes, and Hume: Self-Knowledge, Substance, and Causality* (Madison: University of Wisconsin Press, 1977), 7.

p. 52 "Now you had conceded that if I proved": Augustine, *On Free Choice of the Will*, ed. Thomas Williams (Indianapolis, IN: Hackett Publishing, 1993), 58.

p. 53 "fitting": *ACMW*, 268.

p. 53 "that than which absolutely nothing is better": *ACMW*, 28.

p. 53 "not all of equal value"; "For the nature of a horse is better": *ACMW*, 14.

p. 55 "Consider likewise how the devil": *LSA*, 90.

p. 55 "Take a man who has been sunk": *LSA*, 20.

p. 56 "If anyone doubts whether Anselm": *LSA*, 28.

p. 56 "feeling that he would not escape": *LSA*, 121.

p. 56 "Instantly you might have seen flames": *LSA*, 125.

p. 58 "I began to compose a letter"; "those contemporary logicians": *ACMW*, 237.

p. 59 "used concubines": quoted in *The Oxford Illustrated History of Britain*, ed. Kenneth O. Morgan (Oxford: Oxford University Press, 1984), 114.

p. 60 "No one, after he has become dead": *LSA*, 77.

p. 60–61 "You once said that you wished"; "You loved Count Alan Rufus, and he you": quoted in *SAPL*, 263.

CHAPTER 3: CANTERBURY TALES

p. 64 "When Anselm heard this"; "He was seized": *LSA*, 65.

p. 65 "obedience and necessity": *LSA*, 66.

p. 65 "thank-offering": *LSA*, 67.

p. 66 "The king listened to all this": *LSA*, 69.

p. 67 "As a bishop he ought to have": *LSA*, 69.

p. 67 "The king's mind was worked up": *LSA*, 70.

p. 67 "attacked and torn to pieces": *LSA*, 70.

p. 68 "The long drawn-out dispute": *LSA*, 93.

p. 69 "We consider him as a master": *LSA*, 105.

p. 72 "the liberty of the church": *SAPL*, 278.

p. 73 "the king gave me the archbishopric": quoted in *SAPL*, 250.

p. 77 "was frequently remarked on": *LSA*, 143 n.2.

CHAPTER 4: THE FRIARS OF OXFORD

p. 83 "Intellect more than anything": *The Complete Works of Aristotle*, vol. 2, rev. Oxford Translation, ed. trans. Jonathan Barnes (Princeton: Princeton University Press, 1984), 1862. From *Nicomachean Ethics*.

p. 83 "[n]othing existed at all.": *The Complete Works of Aristotle*, vol. 1, 314. From *Sophistical Refutations*.

p. 83 "It is not possible to untie a knot": *The Complete Works of Aristotle*, vol. 2, 1572–73.

p. 86 fourteen other medieval thinkers: the figure is given in Charles Hartshorne, *Anselm's Discovery: A Re-Examination of the Ontological Proof for God's Existence* (Chicago: Open Court, 1965), 154.

p. 88 "Yet, granted, that everyone understands": *Basic Writings of Saint Thomas Aquinas*, vol. 1, ed. Anton C. Pegis (New York: Random House, 1941), 20

p. 89 "We can demonstrate the existence of God": *Basic Writings*, vol. 1, 21.

p. 93 "besought Master Robert Grosseteste": quoted in Edward Hutton, *The Franciscans in England, 1224–1538* (London: Constable & Co., Ltd., 1926), 124–25.

p. 94 "unless he had graduated in Arts": quoted in Hutton, *The Franciscans*, 130.

p. 94 "he had first lectured on the four books": quoted in Hutton, *The Franciscans*, 129.

p. 95 "will get nowhere with heathen philosophers": quoted in Richard Cross, *Duns Scotus* (New York: Oxford University Press, 1999), 11.

p. 96 "it is altogether necessary to salvation": quoted in Richard P. McBrien, *Lives of the Pope: The Pontiffs from St. Peter to John Paul II* (San Francisco: HarperSanFrancisco, 1997), 231.

p. 97 "no pure truth"; "nothing is in the intellect": quoted in David Knowles, *The Evolution of Medieval Thought* (Baltimore: Helicon Press, 1962), 303.

p. 98 "simpler than the concept of good being": quoted in *The Cambridge Companion to Duns Scotus*, ed. Thomas Williams (Cambridge: Cambridge University Press, 2002), 249.

p. 99 "a more perfect and immediate": quoted in *The Oxford Companion to Philosophy*, ed. Ted Honderich (New York: Oxford University Press, 1995), 209.

CHAPTER 5: OCKHAM'S RAZOR

p. 105 "principal adversary": Marilyn McCord Adams, *William Ockham, vol. 1*. (Notre Dame, Indiana: University of Notre Dame, 1987), 29.

p. 107 "absolutely false and absurd": quoted in Adams, *Ockham, vol. 1*, 30:

p. 107 "This I say"; "that no universal": quoted in David Knowles, *The Evolution of Medieval Thought* (Baltimore: Helicon Press, 1962), 322.

p. 108 "Nothing must be affirmed": quoted in *OPW*, xx.

p. 108 "We must not affirm that something": quoted in *OPW*, xx.

p. 108–109 "What can be explained by the assumption": quoted in *OPW*, xxi.

p. 110 "whether intuitive cognition": *OPW*, 25.

p. 110 "Even if a thing has been destroyed": quoted in Knowles, *The Evolution of Medieval Thought*, 323–24.

p. 110 "Intuitive cognition of a non-existent object": *OPW*, 25.

p. 111 "We could go on *ad infinitum*": *OPW*, 126.

p. 111 "I say that neither the divine essence": quoted in Sharon M. Kaye and Robert M. Martin, *On Ockham* (Belmont, CA: Wadsworth, 2001), 50.

p. 111 "There is no way…of knowing with clear certainty": quoted in Knowles, *The Evolution of Medieval Thought*, 323.

CHAPTER 6: THE NOMINALIST TERROR

p. 123 "O Emperor, defend me with your sword": *OPW*, xv.

p. 124 "constitutional liberal": Arthur Stephen McGrade, *The Political Thought of William of Ockham: Personal and Institutional Principles* (Cambridge: Cambridge University Press, 1974), 37.

p. 125 "that the Emperor has no authority": quoted in *OPW*, xv.

p. 128 "show diligence and zeal in understanding": quoted in Arthur Human and James J. Walsh, eds. *Philosophy in the Middle Ages: The Christian, Islamic, and Jewish Traditions* (Indianapolis: Hackett Publishing, 1973), 604–5.

p. 131 "What do I know?": quoted in Anne Hartle, *Michel de Montaigne: Accidental Philosopher* (Cambridge: Cambridge University Press, 2003), 15.

CHAPTER 7: DESCARTES'S DREAM

p. 134 "Finding no conversation to divert me": *PWD1*, 116.

p. 134 "full of enthusiasm": quoted in *DAB*, 59.

p. 135 "What road in life": *PWD1*, 4.

p. 135 "May God grant that we may live": quoted in *DAB*, 48.

p. 137 "in matters of importance": quoted in *DAB*, 20.

p. 138 "Actors, taught not to let": *PWD1*, 2.

p. 139 "As soon as I completed the course": *PWD1*, 113.

p. 140 "roam[ed] about in the world": *PWD1*, 125.

p. 140 "great book of the world": *PWD1*, 115.

p. 140 "He lives well who is well hidden": quoted in Stephen Gaukroger,
      Descartes: An Intellectual Biography (Oxford: Clarendon Press, 1997),
      292. In addition to Clarke's *Descartes: A Biography* (DAB), I have
      relied on Gaukroger's interpretation of Descartes's life.

p. 140 "never to accept anything"; "nothing more in my judgements":
      PWD1, 120.

p. 140 "devote my whole life to cultivating": *PWD1*, 124.

p. 140 *Admirable and General Method*; *Twenty Books*; *New Astronomy*: *DAB*,
      53, 55, 57.

p. 141 "My whole aim was to reach": *PWD1*, 125.

p. 142 "nothing is known": quoted in *DAB*, 74.

p. 142–143 "I do not want to construct a Lullian": "completely new science":
      quoted in *DAB*, 45.

p. 144 "filled the air of the universe": quoted in *DAB*, 250.

p. 144 "better established, more true": quoted in *DAB*, 83.

p. 145 "distancing myself from my acquaintances": quoted in *DAB*, 436. n.3.

p. 146 "little treatise": quoted in *WOW*, x.

p. 146–147 "[set] out to prove the existence of God": quoted in *WOW*, x.

p. 147 "demonstrate metaphysical truths"; "The first nine months": quoted
      in *DAB*, 101.

p. 148 "Instead of explaining a single phenomenon": quoted in *WOW*, xi.

p. 148 "going very slowly": quoted in *WOW*, xii.

p. 148 "now studying chemistry": quoted in *WOW*, xii.

p. 148 "countless different things": quoted in *WOW*, xii.

p. 148 "give a true account without doing violence": quoted in *WOW*, xii.

p. 148 "the fable of my *World*": quoted in *DAB*, 106.

p. 149 "God imparted various motions": *PWD1*, 240.

p. 150 "thinking substance": *PWD1*, 211.

p. 151 "clear and distinct": *PWD1*, 130.

p. 152 "natural light of reason"; "cannot err on dogmas": quoted in *WOW*, xxvii.

p. 152 "I nearly decided to burn": *WOW*, xxvii.

p. 152 "I must admit that"; "I prefer to suppress": quoted in *WOW*, xxvii.

CHAPTER 8: "A THINKING SUBSTANCE"

p. 156 "And observing that this truth '*I am thinking*'": *PWD1*, 127.

p. 156 "So there remained only the possibility": *PWD1*, 128.

p. 157 "There had of necessity to be": *PWD1*, 128.

p. 157 "imaginary spaces"; "new world": *PWD1*, 130.

p. 157–158 "someone else"; "I had noticed nothing"; "treatise that I had previously intended"; "have an interest in my"; "shocked"; "I do not apologize": *PWD1*, 142, 139, 147, 150.

p. 158 "the one person who has shaken": quoted in *DAB*, 12.

p. 158 "somewhat similar"; "I use it to show": quoted in *DAB*, 210.

p. 158 "is entirely distinct from the body": *PWD1*, 127.

p. 159 "some malicious demon": *PWD2*, 15.

p. 160 "thinking thing": *PWD1*, 195.

p. 160 "cannot come from nothing": *PWD2*, 29.

p. 160 "Existence can no more be separated from": *PWD2*, 46.

p. 160–161 "For I am not free to think of God without": *PWD2*, 46.

p. 162 "to war": quoted in *DAB*, 218.

p. 163–164 "no universality outside of thoughts"; "all universality lies"; "men do not know"; "all the things which are in the world": quoted in David Sepksoki, "Nominalism and constructivism in seventh-century mathematical philosophy," *Historia Mathematica* 32 (2005): 39–40.

p. 164 "You place existence among the Divine": quoted in *TOA*, 46.

p. 165 "Hence the existence of a triangle": quoted in *TOA*, 49.

p. 165 "Oh, Mind": quoted in *DAB*, 204–5.

p. 165 "splendid Platonic things": quoted in Sepkoski, "Nominalism," 43.

p. 165 "Oh, Flesh"; "but even as Stone, Lead, etc.": quoted in *DAB*, 205, 277.

p. 166 "lacks all modesty"; "All I ask for is peace": quoted in *DAB*, 218.

p. 167 "lying biped": quoted in *DAB*, 235.

p. 168 "Thus the whole of philosophy is like a tree": *PWD1*, 186.

p. 169 "things"; "eternal truths": *PWD1*, 208.

p. 169 "these results of mine will be": *PWD1*, 290.

p. 169 "all these opinions to the authority": *PWD1*, 291.

p. 170 "innocent"; "the views that are taught": quoted in *DAB*, 287.

p. 170 "I have got 20 years older": quoted in *DAB*, 305.

p. 170 "hermitage": quoted in *DAB*, 303.

p. 171 "This is my library!": quoted in *DAB*, 304.

p. 171 "the Huguenots hate me": quoted in *DAB*, 180.

p. 172 "I will try here to explain the manner": *The Correspondence Between Princess Elisabeth of Bohemia and René Descartes*, ed. trans. Lisa Shapiro (Chicago: University of Chicago Press, 2007), 65.

p. 172 "ignorant and intractable person"; "very humble and obedient servant": Shapiro, *The Correspondence*, 61, 67.

p. 173 "This is why I ask you": Shapiro, *The Correspondence*, 62.

p. 173 "apply different names to those substances": quoted in *DAB*, 258.

p. 174 "do any better"; "its title may": quoted in *DAB*, 388.

p. 174 "soul has its principal seat": *PWD1*, 341.

p. 176 "fatal conclusion of the tragedies of England": *The Philosophical Writings of Descartes: The Correspondence*, vol. 3, ed. trans. John Cottingham, et al. (Cambridge: Cambridge University Press, 1984), 367.

p. 176 "power and virtue": quoted in *DAB*, 309.

p. 177 "be capable of giving her any satisfaction": *The Philosophical Writings of Descartes: The Correspondence*, vol. 3, 383.

p. 177 "I am not in my element"; "the most powerful kings": quoted in *DAB*, 405.

p. 178 "O, Nature mourn": quoted in *DAB*, 409.

p. 178 "on his way to the army": quoted in *The Cambridge Companion to Descartes*, ed. John Cottingham (Cambridge: Cambridge University Press, 1992), 30–31.

CHAPTER 9: THE ONTOLOGICAL ARGUMENT

p. 181 "Great Scott"; "I saw in a flash": quoted in *The Philosophy of Bertrand Russell*, ed. Paul Arthur (Evanston, IL: Northwestern University Press, 1944), 10.

p. 182 "Modern logic has proved"; "it is easier to feel convinced": *HWP*, 787, 586.

p. 182 "assuming that God is possible, he exists": quoted in *TOA*, 54.

p. 182–183 "I showed this reasoning": quoted in *TOA*, 56.

p. 183 "Whatever we conceive as existent": David Hume, *Dialogues Concerning Natural Religion* (New York: Penguin Books, 1990), 99.

p. 184 "To reflect on any thing simply": David Hume, *A Treatise on Human Nature*, vol. 1 (Oxford: Clarendon Press, 1896), 86.

p. 184 "A hundred real thalers": quoted in *TOA*, 61.

p. 185 "What may be and must be, is": quoted in *HWP*, 417.

p. 185–186 "When I was young": quoted in *The Philosophy of Bertrand Russell*, 19.

p. 186 "mathematical party": *HWP*, 828.

p. 186 "It is here that I have found Occam's": quoted in *The Philosophy of Bertrand Russell*, 14.

p. 187 "It is not an altogether pleasant": quoted in David Edmonds and John Eidinow, *Wittgenstein's Poker: The Story of a Ten-Minute Argument Between Two Great Philosophers* (New York: Ecco, 2001), 51–52.

p. 187 "This language-game is played": Ludwig Wittgenstein, *Philosophical Investigations* (Malden, MA: Blackwell Publishing, 2001), 143.

p. 188 "I do not myself believe": *HWP*, 835.

p. 189 "freshness"; "discoverer and explorer": *HWP*, 557, 558.

p. 189 "the most important schoolman"; "By insisting on": *HWP*, 468, 475.

p. 189–190 "its naked logical purity"; "Clearly an argument with such": *HWP*, 418.

p. 190 "There is no reason to accept": Jonathan Barnes, *The Ontological Argument* (London: Macmillan Press Ltd., 1972), 80.

EPILOGUE

p. 192 "metaphysical head": David Hume, *Dialogues Concerning Natural Religion* (New York: Penguin Books, 1990), 102.

p. 192 "If a word means something": Bertrand Russell, *My Philosophical Development* (New York: Routledge, 1995), 49.

PHOTO CREDITS

1. Photo by Walter Meayers Edwards/NATIONAL GEOGRAPHIC IMAGE COLLECTION/Getty Images.

2. © Nik Wheeler/CORBIS. Detail from the Bayeux Tapestry, an embroidered linen dating around 1080. Bayeux, Normandy, France.

3. Bibliotheque Nationale, Paris, France/The Bridgeman Art Library. The Consecration of the Church at Cluny by Pope Urban II, 1095. Twelfth-century French School on vellum. Ms Lat 17716 fol.91.

4. Bibliotheque Nationale, Paris, France/Lauros/Giraudon/The Bridgeman Art Library. Plan and elevation of Cluny Abbey (engraving) by Pierre Giffart (1638–1723).

5. © Bettmann/CORBIS. Colored etching (1864) of King Rufus and Anselm.

6. © Littlemore Anselm Manuscript, 12th century, Bodleian Library, University of Oxford. MS Auct. D.2.6, FO. 185v. Anselm giving books to Countess Matilda of Tuscany.

7. Courtesy of the Royal Library, Copenhagen. Page from Eadmer's *Life of Anselm*, c. 1200. Manuscript GKS 182 2O: 1R-3OV.

8. Courtesy of Sharon M. Kaye. Color drawing of William of Ockham, sixteenth century. Franciscan Monastery at Kraków, Poland.

9. Courtesy of the Library of Congress. Illustration of monks in William of Ockham's *Dialogus*, c. 1494.

10. © Sandro Vannini/CORBIS. "Triumph of the Catholic Doctrine" fresco by Andrea da Firenze (ca. 1365–1368) in the Spanish Chapel, Santa Maria Novella, Florence, Italy.

11. © CORBIS. Title page of a Thomas Aquinas commentary on Aristotle, *IL Qvator Libros Aristoteles De Coelo & Mundo Commentaria*, 1575.

12. Bibliotheque Nationale, Paris, France/Lauros/Giraudon/The Bridgeman Art Library. Colored engraving of the Jesuit College in La Fleche, 1655.

13. Courtesy of the Library of Congress. Telescope Illustration from Descartes's *Diaptroics* in *The Discourse on Method*, 1637.

14. Louvre, Paris. Lauros/Giraudon/The Bridgeman Art Library. René Descartes, 1649, after the lost original by Frans Hals.

15. Courtesy of the Library of Congress. Illustration of vortexes and a heliocentric universe in Descartes's *Principles of Philosophy*, 1644.

16. Réunion des Musées Nationaux/Art Resource, NY. Photo by Hervé Lewandowski. Detail of a painting by Louis Michel Dumesnil (1680–1746), Chateaux de Versailles et de Trianon, Versailles, France. Queen Christina of Sweden and her court listen to Descartes on geometry.

Index